Standard Test Procedures for Evaluating Leak Detection Methods: Pipeline Leak Detection Systems (UST#45D)

U.S. Environmental Protection Agency

The BiblioGov Project is an effort to expand awareness of the public documents and records of the U.S. Government via print publications. In broadening the public understanding of government and its work, an enlightened democracy can grow and prosper. Ranging from historic Congressional Bills to the most recent Budget of the United States Government, the BiblioGov Project spans a wealth of government information. These works are now made available through an environmentally friendly, print-on-demand basis, using only what is necessary to meet the required demands of an interested public. We invite you to learn of the records of the U.S. Government, heightening the knowledge and debate that can lead from such publications.

Included are the following Collections:

Budget of The United States Government
Presidential Documents
United States Code
Education Reports from ERIC
GAO Reports
History of Bills
House Rules and Manual
Public and Private Laws

Code of Federal Regulations
Congressional Documents
Economic Indicators
Federal Register
Government Manuals
House Journal
Privacy act Issuances
Statutes at Large

United States
Environmental Protection
Agency

Solid Waste And
Emergency Response/
Research And Development
(OS-420) WF

EPA/530/UST-90/010
September 1990

EPA

Standard Test Procedures for Evaluating Leak Detection Methods

Pipeline Leak Detection Systems

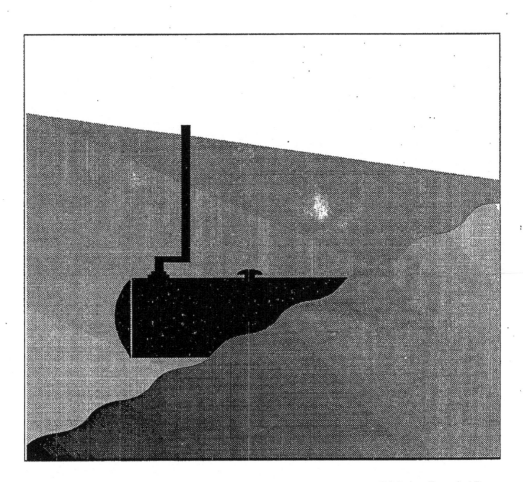

Standard Test Procedures for Evaluating Leak Detection Methods: Pipeline Leak Detection Systems

Final Report

U.S. Environmental Protection Agency
Office of Research and Development

September 1990

DISCLAIMER

This material has been funded wholly or in part by the United States Environmental Protection Agency under contract 68-03-3409 to CDM Federal Programs Corporation. It has been subject to the Agency's review and it has been approved for publication as an EPA document. Mention of trade names or commercial products does not constitute endorsement or recommendation for use.

FOREWORD

Today's rapidly developing and changing technologies and industrial products frequently carry with them the increased generation of materials that, if improperly dealt with, can threaten both public health and the environment. The U. S. Environmental Protection Agency is charged by Congress with protecting the Nation's land, air, and water resources. Under a mandate of national environmental laws, the agency strives to formulate and implement actions leading to a compatible balance between human activities and the ability of natural systems to support and nurture life. These laws direct the EPA to perform research to define our environmental problems, measure the impacts, and search for solutions.

The Risk Reduction Engineering Laboratory is responsible for planning, implementing, and managing research, development, and demonstration programs to provide an authoritative, defensible engineering basis in support of the policies, programs, and regulations of the EPA with respect to drinking water, wastewater, pesticides, toxic substances, solid and hazardous wastes, and Superfund-related activities. This publication is one of the products of that research and provides a vital communication link between the researcher and the user community.

Risk Reduction Engineering Laboratory
E. Timothy Oppelt, Director

PREFACE

Part of a series published by the Environmental Protection Agency (EPA) on standard test procedures for evaluating leak detection methods, this document addresses how to evaluate leak detection systems designed for pipelines associated with underground storage tanks.

How to Demonstrate That Leak Detection Methods Meet EPA's Performance Standards

The EPA's regulations for underground storage tanks require owners and operators to check for leaks on a routine basis using one of a number of detection methods (40 CFR Part 280, Subpart D). In order to ensure the effectiveness of these methods, the EPA has set minimum performance standards for equipment used to comply with the regulations. For example, after December 22, 1990, all systems that are used to perform a tightness test on a tank or a pipeline must be capable of detecting a leak as small as 0.10 gallons per hour with a probability of detection of at least 95% and a probability of false alarm of no more than 5%. It is up to tank owners and operators to select a method of leak detection that has been shown to meet the relevant performance standard.

Deciding whether a system meets the standards has not been easy. Until recently, manufacturers of leak detection systems have tested their equipment using a wide variety of approaches, some more rigorous than others. Tank owners and operators have been generally unable to sort through the conflicting sales claims based on the results of these evaluations. To help protect consumers, some state agencies have developed mechanisms for approving leak detection systems. These approval procedures vary from state to state, making it difficult for manufacturers to conclusively prove the effectiveness of their systems nationwide. The purpose of this document is to describe the ways that tank owners and operators can check that the leak detection equipment or service they purchase meets the federal regulatory requirements. States may have additional requirements.

The EPA will not test, certify, or approve specific brands of commercial leak detection equipment. The large number of commercially available leak detection systems and methods makes it impossible for the Agency to test all the equipment or to review all the performance claims. Instead, the Agency has described how equipment should be tested to prove that it meets the standards. This testing process is called the evaluation, the results of which are summarized in a report. The information in this report is intended to be provided to customers or regulators upon request. Tank owners and operators should keep the evaluation results on file to satisfy the EPA's record-keeping requirements.

The EPA recognizes three distinct ways to prove that a particular brand of leak detection equipment meets the federal performance standards:

1. Evaluate the method using the EPA's test procedures for leak detection equipment.

2. Evaluate the method using a voluntary consensus code or standard developed by a nationally recognized association or independent third-party testing laboratory.

3. Evaluate the method using a procedure deemed equivalent to the EPA procedure by a nationally recognized association or independent third-party testing laboratory.

Manufacturers should use one of these three approaches to prove that their systems meet the regulatory performance standards. For regulatory enforcement purposes, each of the approaches is equally satisfactory.

EPA Test Procedures

The EPA has developed a series of test procedures that cover most of the methods commonly used for underground storage tank leak detection. The particular procedures for each type of system or method are described in a report that is part of a larger series. The series includes:

1. "Standard Test Procedures for Evaluating Leak Detection Methods: Volumetric Tank Tightness Testing Methods"

2. "Standard Test Procedures for Evaluating Leak Detection Methods: Nonvolumetric Tank Tightness Testing Methods"

3. "Standard Test Procedures for Evaluating Leak Detection Methods: Automatic Tank Gauging Systems"

4. "Standard Test Procedures for Evaluating Leak Detection Methods: Statistical Inventory Reconciliation Methods"

5. "Standard Test Procedures for Evaluating Leak Detection Methods: Vapor-phase Out-of-tank Product Detectors"

6. "Standard Test Procedures for Evaluating Leak Detection Methods: Liquid-phase Out-of-tank Product Detectors"

7. "Standard Test Procedures for Evaluating Leak Detection Methods: Pipeline Leak Detection Systems"

Each report on a type of system or method provides an explanation of how to conduct the test, how to perform the required calculations, and how to report the results. The results from each standard test procedure provide the information needed by tank owners and operators to determine whether the method meets the regulatory requirements.

The EPA test procedures may be used either directly by equipment manufacturers or by an independent third party under contract to the manufacturer. Both state agencies and tank owners typically prefer a third-party evaluation, since this is a more objective way of demonstrating compliance with the regulations. Independent third parties may include consulting firms, test laboratories, not-for-profit research organizations, or educational institutions with no organizational conflict of interest. In general, the EPA believes that the greater the independence of the evaluating organization, the more likely it is that an evaluation will be fair and objective.

National Consensus Code or Standard

A second way for a manufacturer to prove the performance of leak detection equipment is to evaluate the system according to a voluntary consensus code or standard developed by a nationally recognized association (American Society of Testing Materials (ASTM), American Society of Mechanical Engineers (ASME), American National Standards Institute (ANSI), etc.). Throughout the technical regulations for underground storage tanks, the EPA has relied on national voluntary consensus codes to help tank owners decide which brands of equipment are acceptable. Although no such code presently exists for evaluating leak detection equipment, one is under consideration by the ASTM D-34 subcommittee. The Agency will accept the results of evaluations conducted according to this or similar codes as soon as they have been adopted. Guidelines for developing these standards may be found in the U.S. Department of Commerce's "Procedures for the Development of Voluntary Product Standards" (*FR*, Vol. 51, No. 118, June 20, 1986) and OMB Circular No. A-119.

Alternative Test Procedures Deemed Equivalent to the EPA's

In some cases, a leak detection system may not be adequately covered by EPA standard test procedures or a national voluntary consensus code, or the manufacturer may have access to data that make it easier to evaluate the system another way. Manufacturers who wish to have their equipment tested according to a different plan (or who have already done so) must have that plan developed or reviewed by a nationally recognized association or independent third-party testing laboratory (Factory Mutual, National Sanitation Foundation, Underwriters Laboratory, etc.). The results should include a certification by the association or laboratory that the conditions under which the test was conducted were at least as rigorous as the EPA standard test procedure. In general this will require the following:

1. The system should be tested on an underground storage tank or associated pipeline both under the no-leak condition and an induced-leak condition with an induced leak rate as close as possible to (or smaller than) the EPA performance standard. In the case of tank or pipeline tightness testing, for example, this will mean testing under both 0.0-gal/h and 0.10-gal/h leak rates. In the case of groundwater monitoring, this will mean testing with 0.0 and 0.125 in. of free product.

2. The system should be tested under at least as many different environmental conditions as are included in the corresponding EPA test procedure.

3. The conditions under which the system is evaluated should be at least as rigorous as the conditions specified in the corresponding EPA test procedure. For example, in the case of tank or pipeline tightness testing, the test should include a temperature difference between the delivered product and that already present in the tank or pipeline.

4. The evaluation results must contain the same information as the EPA standard results sheet and should be reported according to the same general format.

5. The evaluation must include physical testing of a full-sized version of the leak detection system, and a full disclosure must be made of the experimental conditions under which the evaluation was performed, and the conditions under which its use is recommended. An evaluation based solely on theory or calculation is not sufficient.

ABSTRACT

This report presents a standard test procedure for evaluating the performance of leak detection systems for use in the pipelines associated with underground storage tanks. The test procedure is designed to evaluate these systems against the performance standards in EPA's underground storage tank regulations (40 CFR Part 280, Subpart D), which cover an hourly test, a monthly monitoring test, and a line tightness test. The test procedure can be used to evaluate any type of system that is attached to the pipeline and monitors or measures either flow rate or changes in pressure or product volume. This procedure can be used to evaluate a leak detection system that can relate the measured output quantity to leak rate (in terms of gallons per hour) and systems that use an automatic preset threshold switch. The test procedure can evaluate systems used to test pressurized pipelines or suction pipelines that are pressurized for the test. The test procedure offers five options for collecting the data required to calculate performance. The results of the evaluation are reported in a standard format on forms provided in the appendices of the report.

This report was submitted in fulfillment of Contract No. 68-03-3409 by Vista Research, Inc., under the sponsorship of the U.S. Environmental Protection Agency. This report covers a period from March 1989 to March 1990, and work was completed as of July 1990.

TABLE OF CONTENTS

LIST OF FIGURES

LIST OF TABLES

ACKNOWLEDGMENTS

This protocol for evaluating underground storage tank pipeline leak detection systems was prepared by Joseph W. Maresca, Jr., Robert M. Smedfjeld, Richard F. Wise, and James W. Starr for the U.S. Environmental Protection Agency's (EPA's) Risk Reduction Engineering Laboratory (RREL) on Work Assignment 18 of EPA Contract No. 68-03-3409. Anthony N. Tafuri was the Technical Program Monitor on the Work Assignment for EPA/RREL. Technical assistance and review were provided by Thomas Young and David O'Brien of the EPA's Office of Underground Storage Tanks (OUST). Over 50 copies of the first draft of this protocol were distributed for external technical review to petroleum industry trade associations, manufacturers of pipeline leak detection systems, regulatory agencies, and owners/operators of underground storage tank systems. Many of these organizations specifically requested to participate in the review and generously offered their comments and suggestions. A second draft of this protocol underwent technical review by members of the manufacturing, user, and regulating communities attending an EPA-sponsored workshop held in Kansas City, Missouri, in March 1990. This document was edited by Monique Seibel, who also prepared the technical illustrations. Pamela Webster prepared the document for publication.

SECTION 1

INTRODUCTION

A protocol has been developed that can be used to evaluate the performance of leak detection systems or methods used to test the integrity of pipelines associated with underground storage tanks (USTs). The protocol applies to leak detection systems or methods that are physically attached to the pipeline and can relate the measured output quantity to a leak rate associated with the loss of product through a hole in a pipeline under pressure. The system does not, however, have to be one that reports a quantified leak rate. For example, systems that use an automatic preset threshold switch can also be evaluated with this protocol. The performance results are reported in terms of leak rate (in gallons per hour), probability of detection (P_D), and probability of false alarm (P_{FA}). The protocol specifically addresses the performance of these leak detection systems for the leak rates, P_D, and P_{FA} specified in the *technical standards prescribed in the United States Environmental Protection Agency (EPA) UST regulations (40 CFR Part 280 Subpart D)* [1]. The protocol specifically covers all of the *internal* EPA release detection options for piping, but does not cover the *external* leak detection options (those for vapor and groundwater monitoring). A separate protocol has been developed for these external systems [2,3]. Common types of leak detection systems that can be evaluated with this protocol include systems that measure pressure, volume, or flow-rate changes in the pipeline. This protocol addresses both pressurized and suction piping systems and assumes that if release detection is required for a suction system, the line will be pressurized for the test.

The protocol is flexible enough to permit a wide range of approaches to collecting the test data necessary to perform the evaluation and yet is specific enough for the results of each approach to be repeatable. The data needed to perform the evaluation can be collected either at a *special test facility* or at one or more *operational UST facilities,* such as retail stations or industrial storage sites. The same protocol can be used for an hourly test, a monthly monitoring test, and a line tightness test.

Because pressurized pipelines present the potential for a large release of product if a leak occurs, the EPA regulation requires stringent and frequent testing. Methods of release detection for pressurized UST pipelines must handle two different but equally important leak scenarios. In the first scenario, a large release occurs over a short time. The submersible pump that brings product through the pipeline system can pressurize the line for product to be dispensed even though there may be a large hole or fissure in the line. When the line is under pressure, much product can be lost in a short time. In the second scenario, small amounts of product are released over a long period of time; if the leak continues undetected, the net loss of product can be as great as in the first scenario. The EPA regulation for pressurized pipelines require that both leak detection scenarios be addressed. In some instances, the same leak detection system can be used to address each scenario; however, the test procedure, the analysis, and the criterion used to

1

detect a leak may differ. The first scenario requires a test that can be conducted quickly and frequently and that can be used to detect the presence of large leaks having the potential to cause serious environmental damage over a period of tens of minutes to several hours. The second scenario requires a periodic precision test* that can be used to detect the presence of very small leaks having the potential to cause serious environmental damage over a period of a month to a year. The protocol described in this report can be used to evaluate the performance of systems designed to handle each scenario.

The EPA regulation states that "suction piping appears to be intrinsically much safer (than pressurized piping) because product is transferred at less than atmospheric pressure by a pump near the dispenser drawing product from the tank by suction, and failures will result in air or groundwater flowing into the pipe rather than product being released during operation" [1]. As a consequence, the release detection requirements for suction piping presented in the regulation are significantly less stringent than those for pressurized piping. Suction piping is exempt from release detection requirements if the "suction piping meets six design and operating standards concerning pressure, slope, run of the piping system, and use of properly located check valves" [1]. If these six standards are not met, the suction piping system must be tested with one of the monthly monitoring options or must be tested once every three years with a line tightness test. One method of testing a suction piping system is to isolate the line from the tank, pressurize it, and use one of the systems designed for pressurized lines.

It is important to note that in this protocol performance estimates are made in such a way that they can be compared to the technical standards prescribed in the EPA regulation. It should be assumed that the manufacturer will use the best equipment and the best operators (if operators are required) available at the time of the evaluation. The evaluation is not designed to determine the functionality of the system (i.e., whether it operates as intended), nor is it meant to assess either the operational aspects of the system (e.g., the adequacy of the maintenance and calibration procedures) or the robustness of the system.

1.1 TYPES OF SYSTEMS COVERED BY THIS PROTOCOL

Leak detection systems for both pressurized and suction piping can be evaluated with this protocol. The release detection requirements for this piping are described in Sections 280.40, 280.41(b), 280.43(h), and 280.44(a)-(c) of the EPA underground storage tank regulation [1]. The protocol does not specifically include a methodology for evaluating vapor and groundwater monitoring described in Sections 280.43(e) and (f); as indicated above, separate protocols have been developed for evaluating these types of systems [2,3].

1.1.1 Summary of the EPA Regulation for Pressurized Pipelines

The EPA regulation requires two types of leak detection tests for underground pressurized piping containing petroleum fuels. First, as stated in Sections 280.41(b) (1)

---

* A precision test, as used in this protocol, refers to any system that can detect a leak of 0.2 gal/h or better (required for monthly monitoring tests) or a leak of 0.1 gal/h or better (required for line tightness tests).

(i) and 280.44(a), underground piping must be equipped with an automatic line leak detector that will alert the operator to the presence of a leak by restricting or shutting off the flow of the regulated substance through the piping or by triggering an auditory or visual alarm. The automatic line leak detector must be capable of detecting leaks of 3 gal/h defined at a line pressure of 10 psi within an hour of the occurrence of a leak with a P_D of 95% (0.95) and a P_{FA} of 5% (0.05). The test is designed to detect the presence of very large leaks that may occur between regularly scheduled checks with the more accurate monthly monitoring tests or annual line tightness tests.

Second, the regulation also requires either an annual line tightness test or one of four monthly monitoring tests. The annual line tightness test must be capable of detecting a leak as small as 0.1 gal/h (defined at a pressure which is 150% of the operating pressure of the line) with a P_D of 95% and a P_{FA} of 5%. One of the monthly methods allowed is a line test that can detect leaks as small as 0.2 gal/h (defined at the operating pressure of the line) with a P_D of 95% and a P_{FA} of 5%. This option, which is allowed by Section 280.44(c) and described under *Other Methods that Meet a Performance Standard* in Section 280.43(h) of the regulation, requires that the performance of the method be quantified. This quantitative option covers the use of any type of pipeline leak detection system (line pressure monitor, automatic shutdown line leak detector, etc.) that conducts a precision test on the pipeline system and that can satisfy the performance requirements. The monthly monitoring requirement may also be met by one of three other methods of leak detection: vapor monitoring, groundwater monitoring, or interstitial monitoring. The regulation lists specific requirements that each of these three methods must meet. These requirements are designed to assess whether the method is applicable to the local backfill, groundwater, and soil conditions. In general, an engineering evaluation of the site is required whenever a method of leak detection that is external to the tank is used.

1.1.2 Interpretation of the Regulation

The standard for automatic line leak detectors (Section 280.44(a)) requires that a leak of 3 gal/h or larger (defined at 10 psi with a P_D of 95% and a P_{FA} of 5%) must be detected within one hour of its occurrence. This suggests that a test of the line must be conducted once per hour or that the leak detector must be able to sense a leak of this magnitude within one hour of its occurrence.

The automatic line leak detection section of the regulation (Section 280.44(a)) was intended to allow the use of mechanical line leak detectors [4]. Thus, the performance specification in the regulation is identical to the performance claim made by the manufacturers of this type of system. However, this regulatory standard does not preclude the use of other types of automatic systems as long as they can conduct at least one test per hour and detect a release of 3 gal/h (defined at 10 psi with a P_D of 95% and a P_{FA} of 5%); for example, a line pressure monitoring system that has the required performance can also be used.

The regulation also allows automatic line leak detectors to be used for precision testing, provided that the detection systems' performance meets either the monthly monitoring test requirements in Sections 280.44(c) and 280.43(h) - (i) or the annual precision test requirements in Section 280.44(b).

The regulation specifies the minimum leak that a system must be able to detect at specific pressures. Since leak rate varies as a function of pressure, the leak detection test can be conducted at different pressures provided that the determinable leak rate at the specified test pressure is equivalent to or more stringent than the one mandated in the regulation. Examples of equivalent leak rates are given in Table 1.1. (They were calculated from Eq. (4.1), described in Section 4.2.)

Table 1.1. Equivalent Leak Rates

Leak Rate (gal/h)	Test Pressure (psi)	Equivalent Leak Rate* (gal/h)	Equivalent Test Pressure (psi)
3	10	4.25	20
0.1	45	0.07	20
0.2	30	0.16	20

* Based on a theoretical calculation which assumes that turbulent flow occurs through a sharp-edged orifice

1.2 OBJECTIVE

The objective of this protocol is to provide a standard procedure for evaluating the performance of leak detectors that monitor or test the piping associated with underground storage tanks. The type of detector addressed by this protocol is located on a single pipeline connecting the tank with the dispenser. Both pressurized- and suction-piping leak detection systems are included; however, suction pipelines must be pressurized for a test. The protocol can be used to evaluate any leak detection system that can relate the measured output quantity to leak rate (in terms of gallons per hour); systems that use an automatic preset threshold switch can also be evaluated with this protocol. Interstitial leak detection systems can be evaluated with a variation of this protocol, but it should be noted that the protocol is not specifically designed for these systems.

This protocol can be used to evaluate two types of pipeline leak detectors: (1) those that perform hourly tests of the line and that claim to detect leak rates of 3 gal/h defined at 10 psi with a P_D of 0.95 and a P_{FA} of 0.05, and (2) those that perform either a monthly monitoring test with a claimed performance of 0.2 gal/h or a line tightness test (annually for pressurized piping or every 3 years for suction piping) with a claimed performance of 0.1 gal/h with a P_D of 0.95 and a P_{FA} of 0.05. All pipeline leak detection systems will be evaluated for accuracy and reliability for a specified pipeline configuration, under a wide range of ambient test conditions (primarily product temperature), and, at a minimum, at the

4

leak rate specified in the EPA regulation. The probability of false alarm will be estimated at the threshold used by the manufacturer, and the probability of detection will be estimated at the leak rate specified in the EPA regulation.

With one slight difference, the same procedure will be used to evaluate the performance of the monthly monitoring test, the annual line tightness test, and the hourly test. For the monthly monitoring test, the probability of detection will be estimated at a leak rate of approximately 0.2 gal/h, while for the line tightness test the probability of detection will be estimated at a leak rate of approximately 0.1 gal/h; a 3-gal/h leak will be used in the hourly test. The evaluation procedure requires that the performance characteristics of the instrumentation be estimated and that the performance in terms of leak rate, P_D, and P_{FA} be determined for the specified pipeline configuration and a wide range of product temperature conditions. Any automatic line leak detector that can address the 3-gal/h standard will be evaluated under the same range of environmental and pipeline-configuration conditions as the systems that conduct monthly monitoring and line tightness tests. The protocol requires that the operator or system controller calculate and report both the P_{FA} at the manufacturer's threshold and the P_D for the appropriate leak rate specified in the EPA regulation. If it has sufficient performance, an automatic line leak detector used to satisfy the hourly test can also be used to satisfy the monthly monitoring test or the annual line tightness test.

1.3 FOR WHOM WAS THIS REPORT PREPARED?

This report is intended for any person, group, or organization that wants to evaluate a pipeline leak detection system designed to meet one or more aspects of the EPA regulation, and that may in addition want to report the results of such an evaluation. Two groups that will find the report useful are manufacturers of pipeline leak detection systems and third-party evaluators of such systems. Although not specifically intended for regulators or owners and operators of underground storage tank systems, it may nonetheless provide these groups with useful information regarding the requirements for evaluation.

1.4 SAFETY

This protocol does not address the safety considerations involved in evaluating leak detection systems for pipelines containing petroleum products. It is, however, imperative that the leak detection system and the evaluation equipment and facilities be safe and be used safely. Whether the leak detection system is to be evaluated at one or more operational UST facilities or at a special test facility, the organization supplying the leak detection system should provide a standard safety procedure for operating the system and should explain this procedure to the organization doing the evaluation. Similarly, the organization doing the evaluation should provide a standard safety procedure for the use and handling of the evaluation equipment, the pipeline and storage tank facilities, and the product in the pipeline and tank system and should explain this procedure and how to use safety equipment such as fire extinguishers to the organization whose detection system is being evaluated. This should be done before any testing begins. All local, state, and federal health, safety, and fire codes and regulations should be adhered to; these codes and regulations take precedence if there is any conflict between them and the instructions in this document.

1.5 GETTING STARTED

One should read this document in its entirety before attempting to evaluate a pipeline leak detection system. Having done this, one should determine how the evaluation will be conducted and prepare a detailed operational procedure. This is particularly important because this protocol could have been prepared as six separate documents to evaluate the six different types of pipeline leak detection systems covered by this protocol. The particulars of the evaluation procedure depend on which performance standard the system will be evaluated against (i.e., hourly test at 3 gal/h, monthly monitoring test at 0.2 gal/h, or line tightness test at 0.1 gal/h) and whether the leak detection system measures the flow rate and uses it to determine whether the pipeline is leaking, or uses an automatic preset threshold switch and does not directly measure and report flow rate.

There are a number of important choices that the evaluator must make to conduct the evaluation. There are five options for collecting data: (1) at a special instrumented test facility, (2) at one or more instrumented operational UST facilities, (3) at five noninstrumented operational UST facilities where pipeline integrity has been verified, (4) at ten or more noninstrumented operational UST facilities where the status of the pipeline is unknown, or (5) by means of an experimentally validated computer simulation. Of these five, the first four are the most common. The option selected depends on the time and facilities available for the evaluation. The protocol requires that the data be collected on one or more pipeline systems which satisfy a specific set of minimum characteristics established by this protocol, over a very wide range of product temperature conditions representative of those found throughout the United States in all four climatic seasons, and for one or more leak rates that are defined by the EPA regulations; the protocol also provides a means to verify that all of these conditions are satisfied.

Another choice the evaluator must make is whether the test crew and/or the organization supplying the system will have full knowledge of the test conditions beforehand or whether they will be placed in a blind testing situation. In either case, a test matrix of temperature and leak conditions must be defined and data must be collected according to this matrix. The protocol provides a way to develop a test matrix for each type of condition. The protocol is designed to minimize any advantages that the test crew might have because of its familiarity with the tests conditions. Thus, the performance estimates should be identical regardless of whether the test conditions were known *a priori*. Two blind testing techniques are provided that can be most easily implemented at an instrumented test facility; blind testing, it should be noted, takes more time and effort to complete.

Before the evaluation is begun, the vendor must describe the important features of the leak detection system to be evaluated; for this purpose summary sheets are included in Appendix B. Once the system has been defined, the data needed to perform the evaluation can be collected. Three types of measurements must be made. First, the performance

6

characteristics of each instrument that is part of the system must be determined. (This means, for example, the resolution, precision, accuracy, and dynamic range of instruments such as pressure sensors and temperature sensors.) This ensures that the instruments are functioning properly. Second, the data with which to make an estimate of performance in terms of leak rate, probability of detection, and probability of false alarm must be collected. This is the heart of the evaluation, and much of this report focuses on how to collect and analyze these data. This protocol requires that a minimum of 25 leak detection tests *on a nonleaking line* be conducted over a wide range of pipeline temperature conditions. Justification for requiring 25 tests is presented in Section 10 of this report. Additional tests during which a leak is generated in the pipeline system are also necessary. The protocol is designed to use the leak rate specified in the appropriate EPA regulatory standard. Third, the sensitivity of the leak detection system to the presence of small quantities of vapor trapped in the pipeline system must be determined. Only a few tests are required to assess this sensitivity, because a simple field measurement technique is provided that can be used prior to testing to determine whether or not a pipeline contains any trapped vapor. Once these data have been collected, the analysis and reporting procedures are relatively straightforward. The results of the evaluation are to be reported on the form provided in Appendix A. Seven attachments to the evaluation form are provided for describing the system that was evaluated; these can be found in Appendix B.

The protocol specifies certain equipment, apparatuses, and measurement systems to be used in the evaluation. None of these are particularly complex or sophisticated, and a description of each is provided. The protocol allows for the use of other equipment not specified by this protocol provided it has the same functionality and performance as the equipment described.

Only a limited knowledge of mathematics is required to implement this standard test procedure. All of the mathematics can be performed with a calculator or one of the many spreadsheets available on personal computers. This protocol requires that the evaluator be able to:

- sort data from the smallest value to the largest value

- calculate the mean and standard deviation

- fit a regression line to a set of data

- use a random number generator or draw random numbers from a container

- plot and read an x-y graph or be able to linearly interpolate between numbers in a table

The formula for calculating the mean and standard deviation and for calculating the regression line to a set of data is summarized in Appendix E.

7

1.6 UNITS

In this report, the most common quantities are length, volume, time, flow rate, temperature, and pressure. In accordance with the common practice of the leak detection industry, these quantities are presented in English units, with the exception of small volumes measured in a graduated cylinder, in which case the metric units are used and the English units are presented in parentheses. Length is measured in inches (in.) and feet (ft). Large volumes are measured in gallons (gal); small volumes, which are the exception, are measured in milliliters (ml). Time is measured in units of seconds (s), minutes (min), and hours (h). All flow rate measurements made in this report are calculated from measurements of volume and time; flow rate quantities are presented in gallons per hour (gal/h), although the measurements necessary to calculate flow rate will generally be made in units of volume (ml or gal) and units of time (s, min, h) and must be converted. Pressure is measured in units of pounds per square inch (psi). Finally, temperature quantities are measured in degrees Fahrenheit (°F), although some temperature measurement systems used in the leak detection industry employ degrees Centigrade (°C).

1.7 REPORT ORGANIZATION

This report is organized in such a way that it facilitates the evaluation of many different types of leak detection systems against different performance standards and allows the evaluator great flexibility in the approach used for generating the data required to estimate the performance of the system. The report organization is summarized in Figure 1.1. The reason for organizing the report in this way is to make it easier for the evaluator to identify the steps for completing an evaluation (which are presented in Sections 6 and 7) without being encumbered by too much detail. Relevant details are provided in other sections.

Section 1 introduces the protocol for evaluating pipeline leak detection systems.

Section 2 describes the standard procedure for evaluating the performance of any leak detection system in terms of leak rate, probability of detection, and probability of false alarm. As part of the evaluation two histograms are developed: one of the noise that is present during tests on a nonleaking pipeline and the other of the signal-plus-noise during tests on a leaking pipeline. The EPA regulation specifies that certain leak detection systems must be able to detect certain flow rates defined at prescribed line pressures. The flow rate of the leak generated for the signal-plus-noise histogram will therefore be appropriate for the type of system being evaluated (0.1 gal/h for line tightness testing systems, 0.2 gal/h for monthly monitoring systems, and 3.0 gal/h for hourly testing systems) and will be referred to in this report as the EPA-specified leak rate.

Section 3 gives a brief overview of the evaluation procedure that is used to derive the performance estimate. The accuracy of the evaluation procedure and how to assure the integrity of the evaluation are discussed in Section 3.4; the use of other methods of evaluation is discussed in Section 3.5.

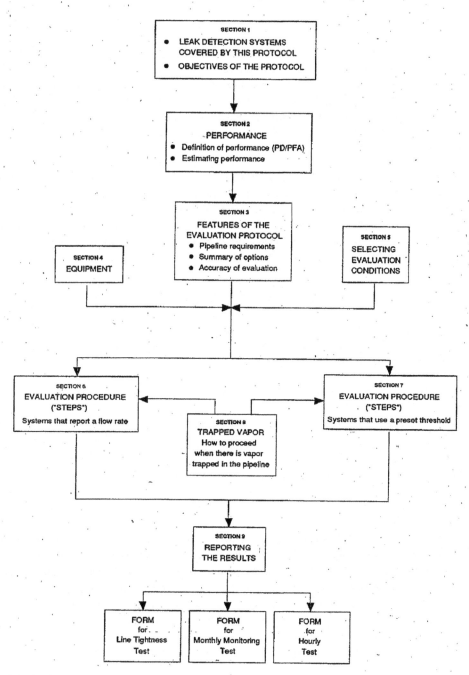

Figure 1.1. Summary of the report organization.

The equipment needed to conduct the evaluation is described in Section 4, including the sensor system and the requirements for temperature and pressure sensors. Section 4 includes a general description of the apparatus required to induce and measure a leak in the pipeline and the various devices needed to characterize the temperature condition of the product in the pipeline, generate a known volume of trapped vapor in the line, and adjust the compressibility of the pipeline system. Section 4 also describes the procedures for making measurements with this equipment. All of the equipment can be assembled with simple mechanical parts. All the equipment can be mounted at existing inlets or outlets so that no new openings in the pipeline are necessary.

Section 5 describes two approaches to selecting and defining the temperature and leak conditions required to conduct the evaluation. In the first approach, the leak rate, temperature condition, vapor pocket, and compressibility characteristics of the pipeline are known by the testing crew before each leak detection test. In the second approach, the test conditions are not known until all the tests have been completed. Both approaches are equally acceptable and will result in identical performance estimates.

Section 6 describes the evaluation procedure for systems that report a flow rate, and Section 7 describes the procedure for systems that use a preset threshold. There are five options for collecting the noise and signal-plus-noise data that are required for the performance calculations. In Sections 6 and 7, a separate procedure is provided for each of these five options. Sample calculations on how to estimate the probability of detection and probability of false alarm are also included.

Section 8 describes how to determine the sensitivity of a pipeline leak detection system to vapor that may be trapped in the line.

Section 9 describes the minimum information required to describe the leak detection system and how to tabulate and report the results of the evaluation.

Section 10 presents the technical basis for the selection of the test conditions.

1.8 NOTIFICATION OF PROTOCOL CHANGES

A draft of this protocol was reviewed by regulators, manufacturers of pipeline leak detectors, providers of pipeline leak detection services, evaluators of leak detection equipment, scientists and consulting engineers, and owners/operators of underground storage tank systems. While the approach used in this protocol has been used to evaluate the performance of underground storage tanks, it has not been widely used for pipelines. Since clarification or modification of the procedures in this protocol may be required once the protocol is implemented by the industry, the EPA requests that any user of the protocol fill out the notification form in Appendix C and mail it to the EPA at the following address:

Office of Underground Storage Tanks
U. S. Environmental Protection Agency
Attention: Pipeline Evaluation Test Procedure
401 M Street, S. W.
Mail Stop OS-410
Washington, D. C. 20460

This will place users on a mailing list so that they can be notified of any changes to the protocol. Comments or suggestions on how to improve the protocol are also welcomed and should be addressed to the same agency.

SECTION 2

PERFORMANCE

To understand how the evaluation is conducted, it is necessary to know the definition of a leak, the definition of performance in terms of probability of detection and probability of false alarm, and how performance is estimated. It should be noted that pipeline configuration and ambient conditions can influence the evaluation.

2.1 DEFINITION OF A LEAK

The flow rate produced by a leak in the pipeline will change with line pressure, increasing when pressure is high and decreasing when pressure is low. The total volume of product that can be lost from a *leak* in a pipeline is the sum of (1) the volume of fluid lost when product is being dispensed and (2) the volume of fluid lost when product is not being dispensed. The total volume of product lost during dispensing is estimated by multiplying the leak rate (defined at the operating pressure of the line) by the duration of the dispensing. Even small holes may result in a release of product at a rate of several gallons per hour. The volume of product lost in the intervals between dispensing is more difficult to estimate accurately. Unless the hole in the line is excessively large, the total volume that is typically released from a leaking pipeline when no dispensing is occurring ranges from 0.03 to 0.06 gal. Product is released between dispensing periods because the pipeline system is elastic, and, under pressure, it expands. At the operating pressures typically found at retail stations, the pipeline system expands 0.03 to 0.06 gal. As the pressure decreases, product is released through the hole at a decreasing rate. Once the pressure reaches zero, no further product is lost. If the hole is very small, the leak may stop before the pressure reaches zero; if the hole is very large, the entire contents of the line may be released.

The values in Table 2.1 illustrate the average monthly release of product resulting from a missed detection, given that product was dispensed at a rate of 5 gal/min to a known number of cars each requiring 10 gal of fuel. The loss of product was calculated on the basis of leaks of 0.1, 0.2, and 10 gal/h, and the averaged missed detections were assumed to be leaks with flow rates that were 50% of these values. It was further assumed that the product was dispensed at 30 psi, that the average volume of product lost in the intervals between dispensing was 0.0264 gal, and that the time between dispensing was long enough for this volume of product to be released. When the leak is small, the quantity of the product released during dispensing is also small relative to the quantity of product released during the intervals when product is not being dispensed. The reverse is true if the leak is large. An average hourly leak rate of 0.1 gal is equivalent to a release of 72 gal per month.

13

Table 2.1. Estimate of the Average Monthly Loss of Product from an Undetected Leak in a Pipeline

Leak Rate	Average Missed Detection	Monthly Throughput	Number of Cars	Product Lost While Dispensing	Product Lost While Not Dispensing	Total Monthly Liability	
(gal/h)	(gal/h)	(gal)		(gal)	(gal)	(gal)	(gal/h)
0.1	0.05	16,000	1,650	3	42	45	0.06
0.1	0.05	50,000	5,000	8	132	140	0.19
0.2	0.1	16,000	1,650	5	42	47	0.07
0.2	0.1	50,000	5,000	16	132	148	0.21
10.0	5.0	16,000	1,650	267	42	309	0.43
10.0	5.0	50,000	5,000	833	132	965	1.34

2.2 DEFINITION OF PERFORMANCE

A complete specification of system performance requires a description of the probability of false alarm (P_{FA}) and the probability of detection (P_D) at a defined leak rate, LR, and an estimate of the uncertainty of the P_D and P_{FA}. These estimates should be made over the range of conditions under which the system will actually be used. They can be made from a performance model based on the histograms of the noise and the signal-plus-noise. The actual calculations will be made with another representation of the histogram called the cumulative frequency distribution.

The *probability of detection* is defined as the number of leaking pipelines that a system would detect if all the pipelines tested were leaking. The probability of detection is expressed as a decimal fraction or a percentage. Thus, a probability of detection of 95%, which may also be written as 0.95, would suggest that the system will correctly declare leaks in 95% of the leaking pipelines tested. *Missed detections* occur if the system fails to declare a leak when one is present; this occurs most frequently when the leak is small compared to the background noise (i.e., the pressure fluctuations that occur in nonleaking pipeline systems, due, for example, to thermal expansion and contraction of the product). The probability of a missed detection (i.e., a false negative) is directly related to the probability of detection. If the probability of detection is 95%, then the probability of missed detection is 5%; if the probability of detection is 99.9%, then the probability of missed detection is 0.1%. The probabilities of detection and/or missed detection are estimated from the cumulative frequency distribution of the signal-plus-noise.

The *probability of false alarm* (i.e., a false positive) is defined as the number of tight (nonleaking) pipelines that a system would declare leaking if all the pipelines tested were tight. Thus, a probability of false alarm of 5% would suggest that the system will incorrectly declare leaks in 5% of the nonleaking pipelines tested. The probability of false alarm can be estimated from the cumulative frequency distribution of the noise once a threshold has been selected.

Detection of leaks in pipeline systems is an example of the classical statistical problem of finding a signal in the presence of noise. In this case, the *signal* is the flow rate of the liquid through a hole in the pipeline, defined at a constant pressure. Note that the primary measurement of the leak detection system may be pressure, or it may be volume, or it may be something entirely different; but it is the leak rate that is the quantity of interest, i.e., the signal. The term *noise* refers to the amount of fluctuation that occurs *in the absence of the signal*. Thus, in order to assess the performance of a leak detection system, one must know the fluctuation level of the measured quantity both with and without the presence of the signal. Noise represents effects that would be misinterpreted (by the particular leak detection system) as a leak when no leak was present or that would mask an existing leak. These are effects that have characteristics similar to those of a leak. Note that the noise is a system-specific quantity. If the leak detection system attempts to detect the presence of the signal (leak) by measuring the pressure drop associated with flow out of the line, then any physical mechanism that produces pressure changes in a nonleaking line and that looks like the pressure changes produced by a leak may be called noise. An effect that is a source of noise for one system may not be a source of noise for another, depending on what measurements are made by the system, the procedure by which they are made, and the analysis that is used to derive leak rate information from these measurements.

The ability to detect a signal is limited by that portion of the noise energy with the same frequency characteristics as the signal (i.e., that portion which could be confused with the signal). The best way to characterize the noise field is to conduct a large number of tests on one or more *nonleaking* pipelines over a *wide range of conditions*. The statistical fluctuation of the noise is observed in the histogram* of the volume-rate results created by plotting the measured volume rates from tests conducted by a given system. The system's output when a leak is present, i.e., the signal plus the noise, can be characterized by means of the relationship between the signal and the noise. If it is not possible to determine what this relationship is, the signal-plus-noise histogram must be measured for each leak rate at which one wishes to know the performance of the system.

An example of the histogram and the frequency distribution for a generic volumetric leak detection system is shown in Figure 2.1. The frequency distribution describes the fraction of the total number of test results in a defined interval. The likelihood of exceeding a specified noise level is described by the integral of the frequency distribution. The resulting cumulative frequency distribution is shown in Figure 2.2. The cumulative frequency distribution is a more useful representation of the histogram because it can be used directly in the performance calculations. If the signal is constant over time and is

---

* Throughout this document, the term "histogram" is used to mean "a graphical or numerical representation of the likelihood that a quantity will be within a range of values." It is easily derived from data and is the primary tool in evaluating system performance.

independent and additive with the noise, the signal-plus-noise histogram can be estimated directly from the noise histogram. For this signal, the signal-plus-noise histogram has the same shape as the noise histogram, but the mean of the noise histogram is equal to the signal strength. An example of the cumulative frequency distribution of the signal-plus-noise histogram for a leak of 0.10 gal/h (flowing out of the pipeline) is shown in Figure 2.3; this is for a volumetric system. Statistical models of the noise and signal-plus-noise could also be developed from the cumulative frequency distributions by means of standard probability distributions, but no models are used in this protocol.

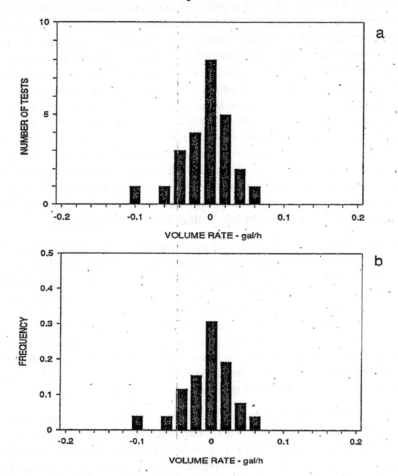

Figure 2.1. Histogram (a) and frequency distribution (b) of the noise compiled from 25 leak detection tests on nonleaking pipelines for a volumetric leak detection system. The mean and standard deviation are -0.003 and 0.031 gal/h, respectively.

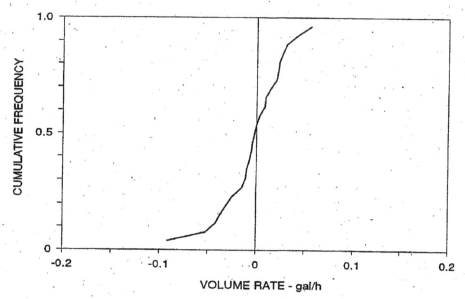

Figure 2.2. Cumulative frequency distribution of the noise derived from the frequency distribution in Figure 2.1.

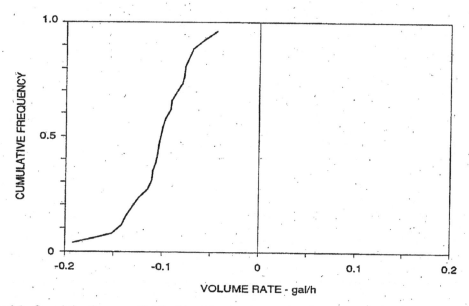

Figure 2.3. Cumulative frequency distribution of the signal-plus-noise generated for a leak rate (i.e., signal) of -0.10 gal/h using the cumulative frequency distribution of the noise shown in Figure 2.2.

Figure 2.4 presents one statistical model, based on the cumulative frequency distributions shown in Figures 2.2 and 2.3, that can be used to estimate the performance of a detection system in terms of P_D and P_{FA}. The noise histogram, represented by its cumulative frequency distribution and centered about zero, shows the volume fluctuation level during tests in pipelines with no leaks. The dashed curve reflects the cumulative frequency distribution of the signal-plus-noise histogram from a pipeline with a leak of 0.10 gal/h. The model shown in Figure 2.4 can be used to determine the performance of the detection system against a 0.10-gal/h leak; the performance against other leaks can be estimated by shifting the signal-plus-noise cumulative frequency distribution accordingly. A leak is declared whenever the measured volume rate exceeds the threshold. For a specified detection threshold, T, the P_{FA} is the fractional time that the noise will exceed the threshold; the P_{FA} is represented by the large dot on the cumulative frequency distribution of the noise. In this example, the P_{FA} equals 0.085. The P_D is the fractional time that the measured volume rate, with the signal present, will exceed the threshold; the P_D is represented by the large dot on the signal-plus-noise cumulative frequency distribution. In this example, the P_D equals 0.945. The probability of a missed detection is $1.0 - P_D$.

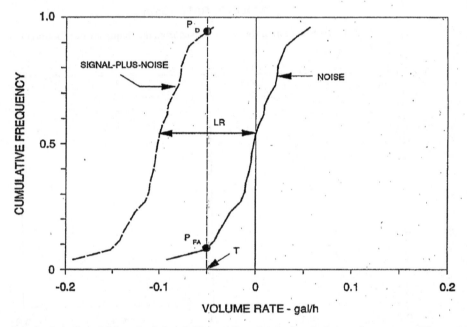

Figure 2.4. Statistical model for calculating the P_D and P_{FA} of a pipeline leak detection system. The model is set up to calculate the performance of the leak detection system against a -0.10 gal/h leak rate. For a threshold of -0.05 gal/h, the $P_{FA} = 0.085$ and the $P_D = 0.945$.

The P_D, P_{FA}, T, and LR are all interrelated; changing one parameter affects the value of one or more of the other parameters. The choice of parameters affects the conclusions to be drawn from leak detection tests (i.e., the reliability of the test result). Once the threshold has been selected, the P_{FA} is determined and does not change, regardless of the leak rate to be detected. The P_D, however, does change with leak rate if the threshold is kept constant. The

P_D increases as the detectable leak rate increases, i.e., there is a better chance of finding large leaks than small leaks. The threshold is usually chosen in such a way that the P_D and P_{FA} present an acceptable balance between economic and environmental risks.

SECTION 3

GENERAL FEATURES OF THE EVALUATION PROTOCOL

The protocol for conducting an evaluation consists of 13 basic steps. Before going into these, however, we first examine how pipeline configuration impacts the evaluation and how various options within this protocol can best be used.

3.1 PIPELINE CONFIGURATION

There is a wide range of pressurized pipeline systems that must be tested periodically for leaks. The leak detection systems used in this kind of testing must comply with the EPA regulation. The performance of many pipeline leak detectors, especially pressure detection systems, will vary according to the configuration of the pipeline system. The magnitude of the signal as well as that of the noise will be affected. This occurs because the overall compressibility characteristics of the pipeline system are influenced by the choice of material (fiberglass or steel), the use of flexible hosing (and its length), and the presence of a mechanical line leak detector* or other appurtenances. For example, the temperature- and leak-induced pressure changes that occur in a static line are inversely proportional to the compressibility of the pipeline system (see [4,5]). This interaction between the pipeline and the performance of the leak detection system presents a challenging problem: the same leak detection system can perform very well on one pipeline system and poorly on another. Fortunately, the compressibility characteristics of the line can be described by the bulk modulus, B, of the pipeline system, where B is the inverse of K, the constant that describes the compressibility of the pipeline system. Two pipelines may have different configurations, but may have the same compressibility characteristics. In this protocol, B, which can be readily measured (see Section 4.3), is used to characterize the pipeline used in the evaluation.

Pipelines constructed at special instrumented test facilities should simulate the important features of the type of pipeline systems found at operational UST facilities. This protocol assumes that the leak detection systems to be evaluated are intended for use on underground storage tanks that are typically 10,000 gal in capacity, where the diameter of the pipe is typically 2 in. and the length is usually less than 200 ft. If the leak the detection system will be used on pipelines with larger diameters or longer lengths, the evaluator should

---

* A mechanical line leak detector is a device that has been used for many years at retail petroleum stations to monitor the pipeline for the presence of large leaks. This device is designed to detect leaks of 3 gal/h or larger defined at a line pressure of 10 psi. The hourly test required by the EPA regulation is based on this device. Because of its wide use and its known effect on the performance of pressure detection systems, it should be included as part the pipeline configuration if the leak detection system to be evaluated conducts a test while this device is in the

21

use a proportionately larger pipeline in conducting the evaluation. Whether the evaluation is conducted at a special instrumented testing facility or at one or more instrumented operational UST facilities, the minimum requirements are as follows.

- The pipeline, which can be constructed of either fiberglass or steel, must have a diameter of at least 2 in. $\pm$ 0.5 in.
- The pipeline must be at least 75 ft long.
- The pipeline system must have a B of approximately 25,000 psi $\pm$ 10,000 psi.
- A mechanical line leak detector must be present within line if the leak detection system being evaluated normally conducts a test with this device in place.
- There must be a way to pressurize the pipeline system.
- There must be a tank or storage container to hold product withdrawn from the line during a test.
- There must be a pump to circulate product from the storage container through the pipeline for up to 1 h. (At operational UST facilities and at most test facilities, this container will be an underground storage tank, and a submersible pump will be used to pressurize the pipeline and circulate product through it.)
- The pipeline must have valves that can be used to isolate it from the storage tank and the dispenser. These valves must be checked for tightness under the maximum operating pressure of the pipeline system.
- The pipeline must contain a petroleum product, preferably gasoline, during the evaluation.
- In addition, when an evaluation is done at a special test facility, there must be a unit to heat or cool the product in the storage container.

When the evaluation is done at five or more operational UST facilities that are geographically separated, it will suffice if only one of the facilities meets these criteria, with the exception of the bulk modulus criterion, which does not have to be met by any of the facilities.

The performance of some of the systems that can be evaluated with this protocol will decrease as the diameter and/or length of the pipeline increases. This is particularly true for volumetric measurement systems that are directly affected by thermal expansion or contraction of the product in the pipeline. The performance estimate generated by this protocol is considered valid if the volume of the product in the pipeline system being tested is less than twice the volume of product in the pipeline used in the evaluation. This is an arbitrary limitation because it does not take into account the type of system, the method of temperature compensation, or the actual performance of the system. It was selected to allow flexibility in the application of the system. Thus, in selecting the length of the pipeline to be used in the evaluation one should consider how the system will ultimately be used operationally. Because the limitation is arbitrary, this protocol also allows the manufacturer to present a separate written justification indicating why pipelines with capacities larger than twice the capacity of the evaluation pipeline should be permitted. Concurrence with this justification must be given by the evaluator. Both the written justification and evaluator's concurrence must be attached to the evaluation report.

22

3.2 SUMMARY OF OPTIONS FOR ESTIMATING PERFORMANCE WITH THIS PROTOCOL

To estimate the performance of a pipeline leak detection system, one must develop histograms of the noise and the signal-plus-noise. Each histogram generated according to this protocol requires a minimum of 25 independent tests. As shown in Section 10.1, this number ensures that an estimate of the P_D of 0.95 and the P_{FA} of 0.05 can be made directly from the data and that the uncertainty in the estimate of the P_D and P_{FA}, as measured by the 95% confidence intervals, is approximately 5%.

This protocol provides five options for generating the data necessary to develop noise and signal-plus-noise histograms. The first option is to conduct the evaluation at an instrumented test facility specifically designed to evaluate pipeline leak detection systems, and the second is to do it at one or more operational UST facilities that are specially instrumented to conduct the evaluation. Both of these options require that the data be collected under a specific set of product temperature conditions, which are measured as part of the test procedure, on a pipeline system that has defined characteristics. The instrumentation is minimal and does not require that temperature sensors be placed inside the pipeline. The next two options require that data be collected over a period of 6 to 12 months, either at 5 operational UST facilities where the integrity of the pipeline systems has been verified, or at 10 or more operational UST facilities. The stations should be geographically located so as to represent different climatic conditions. Each of the operational UST facilities selected should receive a delivery of product to the tank at least once per week. Options 3 and 4 should provide approximately the same range of temperature conditions specified in Options 1 and 2 because of seasonal variations in the temperature of the ground and the temperature of the product delivered to the tank. In the fifth option, a simulation is used to estimate the performance of the leak detection system. This simulation is developed from experimentally validated mathematical models of all the sources of noise that affect the performance of a particular system. These five options for developing a noise histogram are described more fully in Section 6. It is assumed that the first four will be the most commonly used; therefore, the last one is only briefly described.

3.2.1 Generating the Noise Histogram

The primary source of noise for a pipeline leak detection system is the thermal expansion and contraction of the product in the line. Thus, the performance of most pipeline leak detection systems is controlled primarily by temperature changes in the product that is in the line. These changes are present unless no product has been pumped through the pipeline for many hours. In order to take these changes into account, the protocol described in this document requires that all leak detection systems be evaluated under a wide range of temperature conditions.

The range of temperature conditions used in this protocol is based on the results of an analytical study of the climatic conditions found throughout the United States [6,7]. The study estimated the average difference in temperature between the product in the tank and the temperature of the ground around the pipe. The results indicated that values of

±25°F would cover a wide range of conditions. (This is the same range of temperature conditions generated for the EPA's evaluation of volumetric leak detection systems [6,7].) All systems will be evaluated in accordance with their own test protocols under a predetermined matrix of temperature conditions created from an average of the product deliveries and normal dispensing conditions throughout the United States. The protocol in this document describes specifically how to create these conditions.

The performance of most detection systems is also affected by the pressure and volume changes produced by the thermal expansion or contraction of any trapped vapor in the line; in some instances, a leak detection device will simply not work if vapor is trapped in the line. For this reason a significant effort should be made to remove any trapped vapor. Trapped vapor will affect the compressibility of the line and, thus, the magnitude of the bulk modulus. This will, in turn, affect the magnitude of the calibration factor used to convert the measured quantity (e.g., pressure changes) to volume changes. Even the presence of small amounts of trapped vapor can be the source of large errors. The presence of trapped vapor can be determined from the pressure-volume data used to estimate the bulk modulus; vapor in the line should be suspected if the pressure-volume curve is not linear but exhibits second-order curvature, as illustrated in Figure 3.1, which shows the pressure-volume data obtained on a 200-ft, 2-in.-diameter pipeline at the UST Test Apparatus in Edison, New Jersey, under two conditions: (a) with 105 ml of vapor in the line and (b) without any vapor in the line. Since the presence of trapped vapor can be easily checked (see Sections 4.3 and 4.5), this protocol assumes that the leak detection system being evaluated would test the line for vapor and either not test the line or would remove it, if it is present, before a test is begun. As a consequence, all vapor should be removed from the pipeline for all of the tests done and used in estimating performance when the evaluation is conducted at an instrumented test facility (i.e., Options 1, 2, and 5). To assess the sensitivity of the system to trapped vapor, this protocol requires only a few tests to determine the sensitivity of the leak detection system to vapor.

In this protocol, the data used to estimate the bulk modulus will determine whether vapor is present in the line, and three special tests will be made with a small volume of vapor trapped in the line to determine how the system performs under this condition. The results of these three tests will not be included in the performance estimates but will be presented in the evaluation report so that manufacturer's claims about the effects of trapped vapor on the test results can be better assessed.

A histogram of the noise is a requirement for making an estimate of the probability of false alarm. The detection threshold is used to determine the probability of false alarm directly from the histogram of the noise. The histogram of the noise should be compiled from the results of pipeline leak detection tests conducted over a wide range of environmental conditions and pipeline configurations. The tests must be conducted on pipeline systems that are tight. Temperature changes in the product in the line are the main source of noise associated with the type of system likely to be evaluated with this

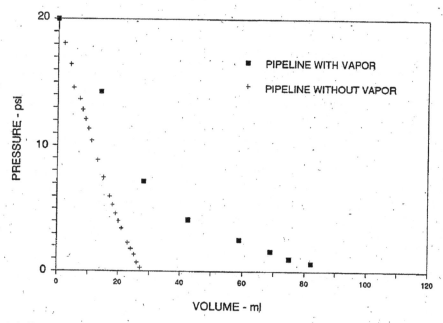

Figure 3.1. Pressure-volume relationship for a 2-in.-diameter, 200-ft steel pipeline with and without vapor trapped in the pipeline system.

protocol. Therefore, a test matrix of temperature conditions has been defined. The temperature conditions are based on those that might be encountered near the end of the day at a moderate- to high-volume retail station.

3.2.2 Generating the Signal-plus-noise Histogram

A histogram of the signal-plus-noise is a requirement for making an estimate of the probability of detection for each leak rate of interest. The threshold value is used to determine the probability of detection directly from the histogram of the signal-plus-noise for a given leak rate. A separate histogram of the signal-plus-noise is required for each signal (i.e., leak rate) for which the performance in terms of probability of detection is desired. For each leak rate of interest, the histogram of the signal-plus-noise must be developed over the same temperature conditions and pipeline configurations used to generate the noise histogram. This protocol requires, at a minimum, that the probability of detection be estimated against the leak rate specified in the EPA regulation for the type of leak detection system being evaluated (i.e., 0.1, 0.2, or 3.0 gal/h). If a signal-plus-noise histogram is developed for a second leak rate, an estimate of performance can be made for a wider range of leak rates, because a relationship between the signal and the noise can be developed.

Generating the signal-plus-noise histogram may be simple or may involve significant effort. There are two options. The *direct* approach is to develop the histogram by generating a leak in the line and conducting a large number of leak detection tests

25

under the same conditions used to develop the histogram of the noise. This direct approach can be used regardless of whether the leak detection system uses a preset threshold or measures the flow rate directly. Noise and signal-plus-noise histograms are required for each temperature condition. In this approach, the histogram of the signal-plus-noise is measured directly for the leak rate at which the probability of detection is desired, and thus the relationship between signal and noise is determined directly. If the duration of the leak detection test is short, the data necessary to develop the noise and signal-plus-noise histograms can be acquired by conducting two tests in succession. The direct approach is most beneficial when a P_D is required for only a few leak rates; otherwise, the time required to collect the data can be excessive. This approach is easy to implement when data are collected at an instrumented test facility or one or more instrumented operational UST facilities, but it is cumbersome if the data must be collected over an extended period at many noninstrumented operational UST facilities. If the probability of detection is required for a large number of leak rates or if the test duration is sufficiently long that only one leak detection test can be conducted for a given temperature condition, the second approach would be more logical.

The second approach is to develop a signal-plus-noise histogram from the histogram of the noise by developing a theoretical relationship between the signal and the noise. An experimentally validated model that gives the relationship between the signal and each source of noise must be developed. With this model and the histogram of the noise, the signal-plus-noise histogram can be developed for any leak rate, and an estimate of the probability of detection can be made for any leak rate. This relationship must be valid over the range of test conditions and pipeline configurations covered by the evaluation. It can be used with all five of the options for data collection. It is particularly useful for evaluating the performance of leak detection systems that require long tests or long waiting periods or that acquire the noise data at many operational UST facilities over a long period of time.

Developing the relationship between the signal and the noise can be difficult if these two phenomena are coupled (i.e., if the noise affects the magnitude of the signal). This occurs, for example, if the pressure, volume or flow-rate changes produced by a leak do not add in a one-to-one manner with the pressure, volume or flow-rate changes produced by each noise source (e.g., temperature changes of the product in the pipeline). If the signal does add linearly with the noise, such a relationship is easily developed by fitting a curve to a plot of the output of the measurement system versus the actual leak rate for two or more leaks generated under benign noise conditions. This curve gives the relationship between the output of the measurement system and the flow rate due to a leak. If the leak detection system is one that measures volume, developing the relationship between the signal and the noise is relatively straightforward, because the volume changes produced by thermal expansion or contraction usually add to those produced by a leak. If, however, the system is one that measures pressure, developing this relationship is more difficult, especially when thermal changes in the product are not compensated for. Not only do the measurements have to be converted from units of

26

pressure to units of volume, but the relationship between pressure and volume is not constant; it changes with pipeline configuration and may also change as a function of the time elapsed since the last change of pressure in the pipeline.

A detailed explanation of how to develop the relationship between the signal and the noise will not be presented here; there are many ways to develop the relationship and many to verify that the relationship is correct. It is up to the manufacturer of the leak detection system to do this. This protocol requires that the relationship be verified with a simple measurement procedure, which is described in Section 4.2.3. This procedure should be undertaken before the noise data are collected. If the relationship has not been verified, the signal-plus-noise histogram must be developed directly during the evaluation procedure.

3.2.3 Generating Histograms with Leak Detection Systems that Use a Multiple-test Strategy

There are many possible schemes for implementing a multiple-test strategy. A leak may be declared if the threshold is exceeded in a certain number of test sequences, for example, one out of two, two out of two, or two out of three test sequences, any other m-out-of-n scheme, or the average of two or more tests. These are only a few examples. The most common multiple-test strategy is to conduct a second test only if the threshold is exceeded in the first test. The critical factor is that the data used to build the histograms *must* come from that test sequence which was the basis for declaring a leak. For example, when a second test is conducted only if the threshold is exceeded during the first test, this means the last test in the sequence; if the threshold is not exceeded the first and last tests are by definition the same. When two or more tests are always required, this means the smallest test result out of the n tests conducted or the average of all of the tests. In addition to histograms used to develop a performance estimate of the system, a second performance estimate is requested. This second estimate is based only on the results of the first test in the multiple-test sequence.

3.3 CONDUCTING THE EVALUATION

The protocol, which is summarized below, requires that a leak detection system be evaluated under a wide range of pipeline configurations and test conditions. It can be used to evaluate systems that require multiple tests as well as those based on a single test.

Step 1 - Describe the leak detection system. The first step in an evaluation is to specify the important features of the leak detection system. This step is important for three reasons. First, a brief description will identify the system as the one that was evaluated. Second, changes to the system may be made at a later date, but the manufacturer may not feel that the changes are important enough for him to rename the system. Such changes may affect the performance, either for better or worse. If the characteristics of the system have been specified in a brief descriptive statement, the owner/operator of an underground storage tank system will have a way to determine whether the detection system he is using is actually the one that was evaluated. Third, the owner/operator will be able to interpret the results of the evaluation more easily if he has this information.

The description of the leak detection system need not be excessively detailed, and proprietary information about the system is not required. The description should, however, include the important features of the instrumentation, the test protocol, and detection criterion. If the system requires multiple tests before a leak is declared, this should be clearly stated. A summary sheet on which to describe the system is provided as Attachment 1 in Appendix B.

Step 2 - Select an evaluation option. The second step is to determine which one of the five evaluation options will be used: test facility, one or more instrumented operational UST facilities, 6- to 12-month data collection effort at 5 operational UST facilities at which pipeline integrity has been verified, 6- to 12-month data collection effort at 10 or more operational UST facilities, or validated computer simulation.

Step 3 - Select temperature and leak conditions for evaluation. The third step is to define the temperature and leak conditions under which the evaluation will be performed. If the evaluation is done at a test facility, at one or more instrumented operational UST facilities, or by computer simulation, the temperature conditions necessary to compile the noise histogram will be developed according to a test matrix, which is generated before the data collection begins, and verified by means of specific diagnostic ground and product measurements made immediately before the test. A matrix of leak conditions will also be generated so that a histogram of the signal-plus-noise can be compiled; the type of test matrix will depend on whether the leak rates are known *a priori* or whether a blind-testing procedure is used.

If the data are collected at operational UST facilities over a period of 6 to 12 months, temperature conditions do not need to be artificially generated, but the relationship between the measured quantity and the flow rate that would be produced by a leak at the manufacturer's standard test pressure (i.e., the relationship between the signal and the noise) should be defined and provided by the manufacturer before an evaluation of the system is performed. This relationship is used to generate the signal-plus-noise histogram from the noise histogram at the EPA-specified leak rate. The relationship can be either a theoretical one that has been validated experimentally or an empirical one that has been developed through experimentation.

Step 4 - Assemble equipment and diagnostic instrumentation. The fourth step is to assemble the equipment needed for the evaluation and to calibrate diagnostic instrumentation such as pressure and temperature sensors.

Step 5 - Verify the integrity of the pipeline system. Conducting a performance evaluation of a leak detection system requires a nonleaking pipeline. If the pipeline is not tight, the performance of the system being evaluated will be degraded. For all but one of the evaluation options (Option 4) presented in this protocol, it is recommended, though not required, that the integrity of the pipeline be verified beforehand with a leak detection system whose performance is already known.

Step 6 - Determine the characteristics of the pipeline system. The sixth step is to determine whether the pipeline system used in the evaluation meets the minimum specified conditions. The same pipeline configuration can be used regardless of whether the evaluation is done at a test facility, one or more instrumented operational UST facilities, or by the simulation approach. The compressibility of the pipeline system must be within a specified range; if it is not, a mechanical device can be used to modify the compressibility characteristics of the line for the test. An example of a device that can be used to modify the compressibility characteristics of the pipeline system is described in Section 4.3.

Step 7 - Evaluate the performance characteristics of the sensor subsystems. The seventh step is to characterize the performance of the measurement subsystems (instrumentation). The resolution, precision, accuracy, minimum detectable quantity, and what the instrumentation is measuring (i.e., specificity) must be determined. Also, the flow rate at the threshold must be determined. Although this step is not actually required in order to estimate the performance of the system, it serves two important purposes. First, it indicates, before the evaluation is performed, whether the instrumentation is working according to the manufacturer's specifications. If the instrumentation is not performing properly or if it is out of calibration, the evaluation should not proceed until the problems are remedied. Second, the instrumentation will ultimately limit the performance of the leak detection system. If it is evident that the performance expectations of the manufacturer are more than what the instruments will allow, the evaluation can be stopped before too much time has been invested or too much expense incurred. Furthermore, this step can be completed quickly.

Step 8 - Develop (if necessary) a relationship between the leak and the output of the measurement system. If the relationship between the leak and the output of the measurement system (i.e., between the signal and the noise) is known or has been supplied by the manufacturer and no direct estimate of the signal-plus-noise histogram at the EPA-specified leak rate has been made as part of this protocol, experiments must be conducted to verify the relationship. This step is not necessary if the test matrix requires the conduct of 25 tests at the EPA-specified leak rate (i.e., developing the signal-plus-noise histogram with the *direct* approach).

Step 9 - Develop a histogram of the noise. The ninth step is to develop a histogram of the noise under the temperature conditions specified in Step 3 for the pipeline system specified in Step 6. This histogram, which is needed to estimate the probability of false alarm, is generated from one or more pipeline tests, conducted according to the manufacturer's protocol, for each condition given in Step 3. If the system uses a multiple-test procedure, two histograms are required. The performance of the system, which includes the entire multiple-test sequence, is generated from the data from the test result used to determine whether the pipeline is leaking (in many instances these are the data from the last test in the sequence). Step 9 is the heart of any evaluation. Once the histogram of the

29

noise is known and either the relationship between the signal and the noise is known or a histogram of the signal-plus-noise has been developed, the performance of the system can be estimated.

   Step 10 - Develop a histogram of the signal-plus-noise. The tenth step is to develop a histogram of the signal-plus-noise for each leak rate at which the system will be evaluated and under the same conditions used to generate the noise histogram. If system uses a multiple-test procedure, two histograms are required. The performance of the system, which includes the entire multiple-test sequence, is generated from the data from the test result used to determine whether the pipeline is leaking (in many instances these are the data from the last test in the sequence). This histogram is needed to estimate the probability of detection. It may be a simple matter to generate the histogram, or it may involve significant effort. The histogram of the signal-plus-noise may be measured directly for each leak rate of interest by developing a histogram of the test results when a leak of a given magnitude is present. As an alternative, a model may be developed and validated experimentally that gives the relationship between the signal and the noise. As stated in Section 2.3.2, if the relationship between the signal and noise is known, the noise histogram can be used to estimate the signal-plus noise histogram. This relationship can be difficult to develop unless all sources of noise during the test are compensated for (or unless they are small). A model is required if one wants to know a system's performance at many leak rates that are different from those specified in the EPA regulation.

   Step 11 - Determine the system's sensitivity to trapped vapor. The eleventh step is to determine the sensitivity of the leak detection system to vapor trapped in the pipeline system. To this end, three special leak detection tests will be performed.

   Step 12 - Conduct the performance analysis. The twelfth step is to calculate the performance of the system in terms of P_{FA} and P_D at the EPA-specified leak rate. The protocol is designed so that the P_D and P_{FA} of the system are determined with the manufacturer's threshold at the leak rate and test pressure specified by the EPA regulation (i.e., 0.1, 0.2, or 3 gal/h). If the evaluation is not done at the pressure specified by the EPA, a method is given to calculate an equivalent leak rate at whatever pressure is used. The protocol provides, as Attachment 2 in Appendix B, a summary sheet to be used in reporting a variety of other performance estimates so that the performance can be compared to that of other leak detection systems. If a system uses a multiple-test procedure, the protocol requires a second performance estimate based on noise and signal-plus-noise data from the first test of the multiple-test sequence.

   Step 13 - Evaluation report. The thirteenth and final step is to report the results of the evaluation in a standard format, given in Appendix A. This form has seven attachments, which are provided in Appendix B. The performance characteristics of the instrumentation, the estimates of the system's performance in detecting leaks in the ambient environment, and the sensitivity of the system to trapped vapor will be presented in a set of tables. The test conditions and pipeline systems to which the detector is applicable will also be presented.

3.4 ACCURACY OF THE EVALUATION

The accuracy of the evaluation basically depends on whether the noise and signal-plus-noise histograms were generated under the required range of temperature conditions, whether the test result was influenced by the fact that the flow rate from the pipeline was known, and whether one or more test results was removed from the data set without adequate justification. In general, a performance estimate will tend to be unrealistically optimistic if (1) less than the full range of temperature conditions was used in the evaluation, (2) part of the test protocol was changed, such as the duration of a waiting period or the duration of the actual test, or (3) one or more of the test results was removed arbitrarily. In the first case, because the temperature matrix consists of a range of conditions, the index used to characterize the temperature conditions has an uncertainty associated with it; contributing to the second error is the fact that many of the test protocols for the leak detection systems are not definitive enough or require some intervention on the part of the operator, whose judgment can be influenced if he knows the status of the pipeline during a test; in the third case, an anomalously large test result might be removed simply because it did not match the expected leak rates. Accurate evaluations can best be assured

- by carefully following the evaluation protocol

- by defining the leak detection protocol before the evaluation begins and following it carefully throughout the evaluation

- by using all of the data collected during the evaluation in the performance analysis

The use of, or the failure to use, *all* the data tends to have the most significant impact on the results of an evaluation. Estimates of the probability of false alarm and the probability of detection are made from the test results that comprise the tails of the noise and signal-plus-noise histograms. When only 25 tests are used, an estimate of a probability of detection of 0.95 or an estimate of a probability of false alarm of 0.05 depends on only one or two test results. Improperly removing one of these from the data set can significantly alter the performance estimates. Therefore, once an evaluation is begun, all of the data should be used unless the leak detection system or the equipment at the evaluation facility can be shown to be malfunctioning, or the evaluation procedure is not being properly implemented. If test results are removed from the data set used to generate either the noise or the signal-plus-noise histogram, this must be clearly indicated, explained, and justified in the evaluation report.

The evaluator (either the manufacturer or a third party) has the option of developing histograms of the noise and the signal-plus-noise with full knowledge of the leak rate in the pipeline during a test. Or, he may opt for a blind testing procedure, which in practice requires that the evaluation be done at a test facility or one or more instrumented operational UST facilities. In a full-scale blind test, the actual flow rates and temperature conditions would not be made available to the test crew until the entire evaluation had been completed. With the protocol used here, however, the test crew knows that one of the leak rates will be zero and one will be the EPA-specified leak rate (i.e., 0.1, 0.2, or 3.0 gal/h). The only possibility, then, is a partially blind test, in which the order of the leak rates is unknown or in which a small percentage of the leak rates is different from the EPA-specified leak rate, or both. One of the partially blind testing procedures used in this protocol requires that 10 to 20% of the leak rates be changed without the knowledge of the test crew. If any of these larger test results is arbitrarily removed, the evaluation is declared invalid and must be repeated. (Temperature conditions can be manipulated in the same way as leak rates.) The partially blind test is intended for use by a third party evaluator, but can also be used by a manufacturer.

3.5 OTHER ACCEPTABLE EVALUATION PROTOCOLS

This evaluation protocol is designed to cover most leak detection systems that measure pressure changes or losses in the volume of product in the pipeline. It is consistent with the ASTM practice [8] being developed for evaluating and reporting the performance of leak detection devices used on UST pipeline systems. There may exist leak detection systems to which this protocol cannot be easily applied, or there may be additional variations of this protocol that might be easier to implement. Other methods of evaluating performance which follow the general approach in Section 2.2 are also acceptable providing that the test conditions are at least as stringent as those described here and that the required number of pipeline configurations is at least as great. Alternative methods of evaluation, which are acceptable to the EPA, are presented in the *Preface* of this document.

SECTION 4

EQUIPMENT NEEDED FOR GENERATING
EVALUATION CONDITIONS

The conditions that one must be able to generate or modify during an evaluation are: line pressure, which influences the leak rate; the leak itself; the compressibility of the line; the temperature of the product in the line; and the amount of vapor trapped in the line. Depending on which of the five evaluation options is selected, one or more pieces of equipment may be required: a leakmaker, a mechanical device to modify the compressibility of the pipeline system, a mechanical device to trap vapor in the pipeline system, a pressure sensor, and tank and ground temperature sensors. This equipment should meet the following guidelines:

- It should measure the flow rate due to a leak in the line at a specified pressure with an accuracy of 0.01 gal/h.

- It should measure the bulk modulus, B, of the pipeline system with a precision and accuracy such that B/V_o is known within 0.025 psi/ml, where V_o is the volume of the product in the pipeline.

- It should measure the total volume of product in the line to within 1 gal.

- It should measure the difference in temperature between the ground and the product at the bottom of the tank (which is brought into the pipeline to produce a temperature condition) with an accuracy of 0.2°F.

- It should measure line pressure during the test with a precision of 0.5 psi and an accuracy of 1 psi or better.

This protocol recommends certain equipment and procedures for making these measurements but does not limit the choice of equipment or procedures to these alone. The protocol requires only that the measurements be made within the specified range of precision and accuracy, and under the specified range of conditions.

4.1 LINE PRESSURE

A pressure sensor is necessary to determine the pressure in the line during each test and to set a leak rate. Pressure measurements can be made with either a mechanical gauge or an electromechanical transducer and automatic data acquisition system. A mechanical gauge that has been calibrated is more than satisfactory.

4.1.1 Equipment and Instrumentation for Generating Line Pressure

A mechanical pressure gauge that can be read manually to the nearest 0.5 psi and has an accuracy of 1 psi can be used to measure pressure. To measure pressure

33

automatically, a pressure transducer that has a precision and accuracy of 0.5 and 1 psi, respectively, can be used. Even if pressure is recorded automatically, it is desirable to insert a mechanical pressure gauge in the line to help conduct and control the experimental measurements. The pressure sensor can be attached at any point on the pipeline.

These pressure sensors should be calibrated before each evaluation, or more frequently, if required. Calibration is done by applying a known pressure to the system and recording the output of the sensor. A mercury manometer can be used for this purpose. Calibration data should be obtained in increments of 5 psi or less. At least five points are required. A calibration curve is generated by fitting a regression line to the pressure measured by the sensor being calibrated (y axis) and the known pressure from the reference source (x axis). The precision of the sensor is estimated from the standard deviation of the ordinate (y axis). The accuracy is determined from the intercept of the curve of the leak rate. The calibration curve should be used to convert the output of the sensor to pressure units (e.g., volts to psi); if the sensor output is already in units of pressure, the calibration curve will correct any measurement errors that the sensor may have developed since its original calibration by the manufacturer.

4.1.2 Measurement of Line Pressure

If pressure measurements are recorded digitally by a computer, it is important that the time clocks on all the instruments be synchronized to the nearest second with the clock used in the evaluation, and that the start and end times of all pressure measurements required to complete the evaluation be recorded. If the pressure measurements are made with a mechanical or electrical gauge, the pressures should be read by the tester and the time of the reading recorded.

4.2 LEAK RATE

One or more leaks must be generated during an evaluation as a means of developing a signal-plus-noise histogram. A device is needed that can establish and maintain a leak with a constant flow rate at a given pressure. This can be done, for example, by using a flow meter or by measuring the volume of product that is released over time through a valve or orifice. This protocol shows how a leak can be generated with the latter approach (see Sections 4.2.1 and 4.2.2), but any device will do provided that it is properly calibrated and used. For example, if a flow meter set to generate a particular flow rate is used, the flow rate must be verified experimentally at the appropriate pressures by means of a method similar to the one described in Section 4.2.2.

A leak can be generated at any location in the line. Generally, it is most convenient to withdraw product at either end of the line, i.e., either near the submersible pump and mechanical line leak detector or at the shear valve near the dispenser. The latter tends to be the easiest location at which to generate and measure the leak. This protocol has established a line pressure of 20 psi as the standard pressure for defining a leak rate for all pipeline leak detection systems, with the exception of the hourly testing systems, in which the EPA

34

regulation has established a specific pressure of 10 psi (i.e., 3 gal/h) as the standard for defining the leak to be detected. As a consequence, all values of leak rate will be established at 10 psi for the hourly testing systems designed to meet the 3-gal/h EPA standard and at 20 psi for all other systems designed to meet the 0.2-gal/h monthly monitoring or 0.1-gal/h line tightness testing EPA-standards. When using a leak-making device similar to the one described in Section 4.2.1, the evaluator sets a leak rate by adjusting the size of an orifice, usually by means of an adjustable valve. Once the rate of the leak through the valve or orifice has been set at either 10 psi or 20 psi, depending on whether the system uses an hourly test or not, any other pressure can be used during the evaluation provided that the size of the orifice does not change. For any system being evaluated, an initial test pressure will be stipulated by the manufacturer; it is recommended that the leak rate be measured at this initial pressure in addition to the 10 or 20 psi.

If it is not possible to establish the leak rate at 10 or 20 psi, the appropriate leak rate for the given pressure can be established by means of a mathematical relationship. This mathematical relationship can be used to determine the equivalent leak rate at the test pressure so that the EPA-specified leak rate is properly defined at 10 or 20 psi.

The mathematical relationship required to convert a leak rate generated at the test pressure to 20 psi depends on whether the flow is laminar or turbulent, which in turn depends on the density and viscosity of the product, the diameter of the hole, and the length and roughness characteristics of the leak-making apparatus itself. The relationship describing the flow through a hole in an *in situ* pipeline is even more complicated because the surrounding backfill and any residual sediment in the product will also affect the flow rate. For laminar flow, the flow rate for free flow through an orifice is proportional to the pressure at the orifice; for turbulent flow, the flow rate is proportional to the square root of pressure. Eqs. (4.1) and (4.2) give relationships that can be used to convert the leak rate at the test pressure to the leak rate at 20 psi for turbulent and laminar flow, respectively. These equations can be used to convert leak rate, LR, measured in psi at one pressure, P, to a leak rate, $LR_{20\,psi}$, at a pressure of 20 psi. These two equations should bracket the actual relationship for the pipeline, leak-maker and product.

$$LR_{20\,psi} = LR\,(20/P)^{0.5} \qquad\qquad (4.1)$$

$$LR_{20\,psi} = LR\,(20/P) \qquad\qquad (4.2)$$

This mathematical relationship should be developed empirically for the pipeline, product and leak-making device to be used in the evaluation. This can be done by setting the leak rate of interest at 10 or 20 psi and then measuring the same flow rate through the same orifice at the test pressure; this procedure should be repeated three times to obtain a median value. Once this has been done, the leak rate measured at the test pressure can be used during the evaluation. It is important to note that this leak rate will be different from *but equivalent to* the leak rate measured at 10 or 20 psi.

Sometimes it is not possible to develop an empirical relationship. In such cases a theoretical relationship can be used. If it is not possible to justify experimentally the use of either Eqs. (4.1) or (4.2), Eq. (4.1) should be used. For gasoline motor fuels, Eq. (4.1) agrees well with experimental measurements.

4.2.1 Equipment and Instrumentation for Generating Leaks

To generate the leak described above, the following equipment can be used: a leak-making device that allows a constant flow of product from a pipeline, graduated cylinders, a stopwatch, a pressure sensor, and a 1-gal storage container that can safely handle petroleum fuels. Figure 4.1 illustrates the important features of an apparatus that can be used to generate a leak. A mechanical system that has three valves and that can be easily attached to and detached from the line is required. One of the valves (Valve B) is a metered valve that is used to set the leak rate and release product from the line. This valve should have a dial mechanism that can be used to adjust and maintain a constant flow rate. Another valve (Valve A), located between the line and the metered valve, is used to open and close the line. Valve C is used to release a larger volume of product from the line. One generates a leak at a given line pressure by first pressurizing the line, then opening Valve A and adjusting Valve B until the desired leak rate is obtained.

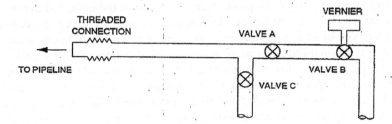

Figure 4.1. Schematic diagram of an apparatus to generate small and large leaks in the pipeline.

4.2.2 Measurement of Leak Rate

The line must kept at a constant pressure while the leak rate is being measured. Normally, this would be the operating pressure of the pipeline during dispensing of product.

Making this measurement requires a number of graduated cylinders, preferably 10 ml, 25 ml, 100 ml, and 250 ml in size. It is recommended that at least one graduated cylinder of each size be available. Note that these cylinders should not be used to *store* product; for safety reasons, a proper storage container should be used to hold product removed from the pipeline during the tests.

The procedure for generating a leak is as follows:

- Bring the line to the pressure required for testing.

- Open Valve A and adjust Valve B until the leak rate of interest is obtained. Then close Valve A until it is time to generate a leak in the line. Open Valve A to generate the leak.

- Using a graduated cylinder and a stopwatch, measure the volume of product released from the line until Valve A is closed. Recommendations for the size of the graduated cylinder and the approximate lengths of the measurements, in seconds, are given in Table 4.1. In general, these measurements will be made in milliliters and will have to be converted to gallons.

- Repeat the leak rate measurement twice and use the median of the three leak rate estimates if the difference between the minimum and maximum values is less than 0.02 gal/h.

- Make additional measurements if the difference between the minimum and maximum values exceed 0.02 gal/h, and use only the last three consecutive measurements to make the calculation.

- Keep the pressure constant to within ±1 psi during the measurements.

Table 4.1. Recommendations for Measuring Leak Rate

Graduated Cylinder Size (ml)	Minimum Graduated Divisions* (ml)	Length of Measurement** (s)	Leak Rate (gal/h)	Error in Measuring Leak Rate (gal/h)
10	0.2	10	0.95	0.009
10	0.2	60	0.16	0.002
25	0.2	10	2.37	0.009
25	0.2	60	0.40	0.002
100	1.0	10	9.50	0.047
100	1.0	60	1.58	0.008

* Read the graduated cylinder to the nearest 0.5 division.
** Record time to the nearest 0.1 s.

The leak rate should be measured each time the metered valve (Valve B) is adjusted. The leak rate should also be checked if testing is done over a period of 1 h or longer at one set leak rate. When the test is long, it is recommended that leak rate measurements be made at the beginning and end of the test period and that the average leak rate be reported.

It is recommended that a calibration curve be developed for the metered valve so that the dial on this valve can be used to set the approximate leak rate. This calibration curve is generated at a specific pressure; five leak rates are generated over the range of interest. A calibration curve can be developed by fitting a regression line to an x-y plot of the dial readings (y axis) versus the measured leak rates (x axis). This curve can be used to help control and simplify the experimental procedure because it allows the evaluator to set the leak rate. The dial should not be used to set leak rates unless the leak-generating apparatus can be shown to have highly repeatable results, i.e., within 0.01 gal/h.

37

4.2.3 Relationship Between the Signal and the Noise

If the signal-plus-noise histogram required by this protocol at the EPA-specified leak rate will be developed directly from measurements made during the evaluation, it is not necessary to identify the relationship between the signal and the noise, and the reader can proceed to Section 4.3.

There are many approaches that can be used to verify that the relationship between the signal and the noise provided by the manufacturer is valid. A complete experimental validation requires that the histogram of the signal-plus-noise be developed for at least three leak rates over a wide range of noise (i.e., temperature) conditions. This, however, constitutes more data than what is obtained by directly measuring the signal-plus-noise histogram at the EPA-specified leak rate. The amount of data that are necessary can be reduced somewhat if the relationship between the signal and noise is based on well-known physical models whose important features can be verified. If the relationship is incorrectly defined, the performance of the leak detection system could be adversely affected; the direct measurement approach, on the other hand, will not be impacted by an incorrect relationship. It is recommended, therefore, that if the relationship between the signal and the noise has not been thoroughly validated before the evaluation, it should not be used, and the signal-plus-noise histogram should be generated from direct measurements.

This protocol requires two simple checks whose purpose is to determine whether the relationship provided by the manufacturer is valid and can be used to develop a signal-plus-noise histogram from the noise data.

The first check determines whether or not the relationship can be used to find the mean of the signal-plus-noise histogram for a given leak rate. It also gives the relationship between the output quantity and leak rate. Leak rates of approximately 0.0, 0.05, 0.10, 0.20, 0.30, and 0.40 gal/h should be used if the system is designed to detect either a 0.1- or a 0.2-gal/h leak rate, and rates of approximately 0.0, 2.0, 2.5, 3.0, 3.5, and 4.0 gal/h should be used if the system is designed to detect leaks of 3 gal/h. The leak should be generated at a constant pressure of 10 or 20 psi, whichever is appropriate. If this is not possible, a leak rate equivalent to the one specified at 10 or 20 psi can be generated at a constant pressure other than 10 or 20 psi. An x-y plot of the output quantity of the system (y axis) and the actual flow rate due to each (x axis) should be made, and a regression line (least-squares line) should be fit to the data. The equation that describes this line gives the relationship between the measured and actual signal when the temperature changes are small. The output of the measurement system calculated from this regression line (at the EPA-specified leak rate) should then be compared to the output derived from the relationship provided by the manufacturer. The standard deviation of the ordinate (y axis), an indication of the uncertainty of the relationship, should also be calculated.

If there were a way of knowing *a priori* whether the signal adds linearly to the noise, this check would be the only one required. Since it is not possible to know this beforehand, both checks must be done. The first check does not assess whether the relationship correctly predicts how the effects of a leak and product temperature changes are combined. If the signal does not add linearly with the noise, the shape of the noise histogram (which might be assessed from the standard deviation of the data) will be different from the shape of the signal-plus-noise histogram, and additional information is required to check the relationship.

The second check verifies the relationship in cases when the temperature changes in the product in a leaking pipeline are not small. It is this step that could require significant effort. In this protocol, however, only a simple check is done; if the manufacturer's relationship is verified by this check, it is assumed that it is valid in general. Three leak detection tests are conducted according to the procedures for generating a temperature condition in Section 5.1. The first test (Test A) is done on a pipeline in which the temperature changes are negligible. A leak equal to the EPA-specified leak rate is generated for this test. The other two tests are done when there is at least a 10°F temperature difference between the product in the pipeline and the temperature of the backfill and soil surrounding the pipeline (these changes should be the same for each test); one of the tests (Test B) is done on a tight pipeline and the other (Test C) is done on a pipeline with a leak equal to the EPA-specified leak rate. When the outputs from Tests A and B are combined according to the relationship provided by the manufacturer, they should be equal to the output from Test C. That is, the leak rate under the given temperature condition should equal the sum of (1) the leak rate when there is no temperature change and (2) a zero leak rate under the given temperature condition when (1) and (2) are properly combined.

There are no specified criteria in this protocol for accepting or rejecting either check. The checks are made and the results are reported. If the checks show that using this relationship will result in a large error, the relationship should not be used. (Errors equivalent to 0.03 to 0.06 gal/h can have a significant impact on the performance of the system against leak rates of 0.1 and 0.2 gal/h, respectively.) The decision to use the relationship is up to the manufacturer.

The results of these tests should be reported in the tables provided in Attachments 3, 4, and 7 in Appendix B. Attachment 7 summarizes the results of the two checks. Attachments 3 and 4 summarize the temperature and leak conditions, as well as the test results.

4.3 PIPELINE COMPRESSIBILITY CHARACTERISTICS

In four of the five evaluation options, the compressibility characteristics of the pipeline system used in the evaluation must be determined. For three of these options, this protocol gives a specific value for the compressibility of the line. The compressibility can be characterized by the bulk modulus, B, of the pipeline system, which can be estimated with a simple measurement procedure.

4.3.1 Equipment and Instrumentation for Modifying Pipeline Compressibility

To determine the compressibility of the pipeline, one needs a pressure sensor, either mechanical or electrical, a leak-generating apparatus, a stopwatch, and a graduated cylinder. If the compressibility characteristics of the pipeline do not meet the specifications of this protocol (i.e., 25,000 psi ± 10,000 psi), there are two choices: use another pipeline system or modify the compressibility characteristics of the pipeline using the device shown in Figure 4.2.

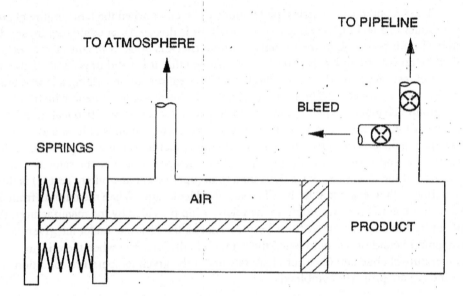

Figure 4.2. Mechanical device to modify the compressibility characteristics of the pipeline system.

The device shown in Figure 4.2 consists of a liquid-tight piston that is installed in a cylinder. Liquid from the pipeline is allowed to enter the chamber in front of the piston. When the pipeline is placed under pressure, the liquid will apply a force on the face of the piston; the springs attached to the back of the piston resist this force. This device will affect the compressibility of the pipeline system. The magnitude of its effect depends on the spring constant.

A device of this type was built and used to modify the compressibility characteristics of the pipeline system at the EPA's UST Test Apparatus. The device consisted of a pneumatic cylinder[*] 2 in. in diameter and 12 in. long, a piston with a stroke of 8 in., and two springs each having an outer diameter of 11/16 in., a length of 4 3/4 in., and a spring constant of 11.9 psi. The device changed the compressibility characteristics of the pipeline by a factor of three.

---

[*] The device that was assembled and field-tested during the development of this protocol was built with a Chicago Pneumatic Cylinder Model DS-96-8-V.

4.3.2 Measurement of Pipeline Compressibility

The procedure for measuring pipeline compressibility is to drain product from a line initially raised to operating pressure, and then measure simultaneously the cumulative volume of product released from the line and the pressure in the line at the time of the volume measurement. The procedure includes the compressibility effects of any vapor trapped in the line. If no vapor is trapped in the pipeline, pressure (y axis) should be linearly related to volume (x axis). The slope of a regression line fit to these data gives an estimate of B/V_o; B can be estimated directly if the volume of the product in the line, V_o, is known. Figure 4.3 is an example of the pressure-volume plot for data collected on a 2-in.-diameter, 165-ft-long pipeline with and without a mechanical line leak detector present. Figure 4.3 shows that the pressure-volume relationship is linear and that it changes if a mechanical line leak detector is present.

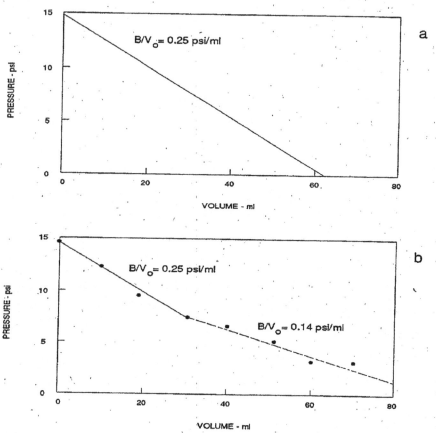

Figure 4.3. Pressure-volume relationship for a 2-in.-diameter, 165-ft pipeline (a) without and (b) with a mechanical line leak detector.

41

Figure 4.4 shows the difference in the pressure-volume relationship in a 2-in.-diameter, 200-ft-long steel pipeline when the compressibility device is attached to the line and when it is not. If vapor is trapped in the pipeline, the pressure-volume relationship will not be linear but will exhibit curvature as illustrated in Figure 3.1. Thus, this measurement also provides a simple way to determine if there is any vapor trapped in the pipeline.

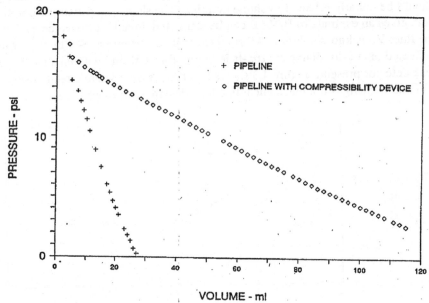

Figure 4.4. Pressure-volume relationship for a 2-in.-diameter, 200-ft steel pipeline when the compressibility device is attached to the line and when it is not.

The value of B will depend on when and how the test pressure in the line is established. If the pressure is raised or lowered suddenly, as typically happens when the submersible pump is turned on, the pressure changes in the line will be adiabatic. If a test is conducted immediately after the pressure has been raised suddenly and if the duration of the test is short (less than 5 min or so), B will be nearly adiabatic. If the test is long (about 1 h) or if the pressure is kept constant for 15 min before beginning a test, B will not be adiabatic and will have a different value.

The pressure measurements are best accomplished with a mechanical pressure gauge, which eliminates the time registration problems that are encountered if volume measurements are made manually and if pressure measurements are made with an electrical pressure transducer and a digital acquisition system. For a given thermodynamic regime (e.g., adiabatic), the value of B or B/V_o should not change as a function of leak rate, so any convenient leak rate can be used in performing the calibration. B can, however, vary with temperature, so these measurements should not be made until the temperature changes in the pipeline are less than 0.01°C. In general, an 8- to 12-h waiting period will ensure that the temperature changes are small. The selected

42

leak rate should be as large as possible while still allowing pressure measurements to be made to within 1 psi and volume measurements to be made to within 1 ml. In most pipelines the total volume of product that will be drained as the pressure drops from 20 psi to near 0 psi ranges from 20 to 200 ml.

The pressure-volume measurements can be difficult to make from an operational standpoint if the leak rate is too large. In general, it takes two people if pressure measurements are made with a mechanical gauge and the cumulative volume of released product is read in a graduated cylinder. The best way to make this measurement is to read the pressure in predetermined intervals of 5 or 10 ml as the graduated cylinder is filling up with product that is draining from the line. For most pipelines, accurate measurements can be made if the leak-making apparatus is set to allow a flow rate of between 0.20 and 0.5 gal/h at the test pressure; the exact flow rate of the leak is unimportant and does not need to be measured. The data collection should be completed in less than 2 min; if the test is completed in less than 2 min, the value of B should be nearly equal to the value of B for an adiabatic process. Enough pairs of pressure-volume data points should be collected so that the slope of the line can be accurately determined. It is recommended that at least five points be used. Three measurements of B/V_0 should be made and the median value should be reported. The differences between the median value and the minimum and maximum values should be less than 10%.

The volume of the product in the pipeline can be estimated if the diameter and length of the pipe and fittings are known. An estimate can be made from final construction drawings that show what was actually installed. The volume of the product in the pipeline should be known to within 1 gal (the amount of product contained in a 6-ft length of 2-in.-diameter pipe, or 10% of the total volume in the line).

4.4 PRODUCT TEMPERATURE

It is very difficult to measure the rate of change of temperature of the product inside a pipeline. To do this would require an array of temperature sensors capable of measuring the rate of change of temperature to 0.2°F. Since two to three uniformly spaced sensors are required for each 10 gal of product in the line, a 100-ft, 2-in.-diameter line would require approximately six temperature sensors. Even if such an array measured the product temperature accurately, there would be no guarantee of standardized evaluation conditions. This is because the temperature of the product in the pipeline changes exponentially over time and the rate of change depends on the heat transfer properties of the pipeline and the backfill and soil surrounding it, as well as on the temperature of the product in the pipeline and the temperature distribution in the backfill and soil at the start of the test. When the dispenser is turned on, product from the bottom of the storage tank, which is at a certain temperature, is pumped through the pipeline, whose surrounding backfill and soil may be at a different temperature. As more product is dispensed through the pipeline, the temperature distribution in the surrounding backfill and soil changes. Thus, the temperature of the backfill and soil immediately surrounding the pipeline may be very different from the temperature of the soil some distance away. The degree of difference depends on how often

43

product was dispensed prior to the test and how long it has been since the last dispensing of product through the pipeline. As a consequence, the actual rate of change of temperature of product in the pipeline during two leak detection tests can be very different, even though the temperature difference between the product in the tank and the temperature of the backfill or soil located far away from the pipeline is the same. Heat-transfer calculations with mathematical models and experimental measurements on UST pipeline systems suggest that the rate of change of product temperature will decrease to less than 0.02°F/h (0.01°C/h) 8 to 12 h or less after dispensing has ceased. Therefore, a leak detection system whose protocol includes a waiting period between the last dispensing of product and the beginning of a test will always experience more benign temperature conditions than a system whose protocol does not require a waiting period. Simply comparing the temperature difference between product at the bottom of the tank and product in the pipeline (or the ground temperature at the same depth as the pipeline but not adjacent to it) is not sufficient, because this difference does not accurately account for the distribution of temperature in the backfill and soil.

Figure 4.5 illustrates the difference in the rate of change of temperature of the product within the pipeline under two different ground conditions. In Figure 4.5(a), the temperature of the ground is constant and in Figure 4.5(b), the temperature of the ground changes as the distance from the pipe increases. In Figure 4.5(b) the initial ground temperature was the same as in Figure 4.5(a); product that was 9°F (5°C) warmer than the ground was then dispensed continuously through the pipeline for 16 h. Figure 4.5(c) shows the rate of change of temperature under both ground conditions; in this instance the temperature of the product at the bottom of the tank was 9°F warmer than that of the ground 12 in. from the pipeline. The rate of change of temperature is clearly different. When there is no dispensing of product through the line, the initial rate of change of temperature is great, but the temperature of the product in the pipeline approaches the temperature of the ground more quickly. This, however, is not typical of what occurs at a retail station. Calculations with a mathematical model show that the rate of change of temperature (of the product) is similar regardless of whether product has been dispensed through the line for 1 h or for 16 h. However, when product has been flowing through the line for only several minutes, the rate of change is quite different.

4.4.1 Equipment and Instrumentation for Generating Product Temperature

In answer to the problem of characterizing temperature conditions, a procedure has been developed that can be used to ensure that all evaluations of pipeline leak detection systems are conducted under similar conditions. Four temperature sensors having a precision and a relative accuracy of 0.2°F are required. The relative accuracy can be determined by calibrating all four temperature-sensors together in the same temperature bath so that each is referenced to the same temperature; in this way differences in sensor readings can be accurately measured and accounted for.

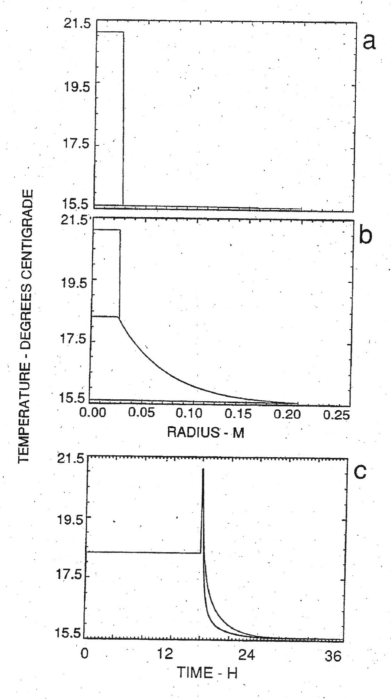

Figure 4.5. Product temperature changes predicted for different dispensing operations using a heat transfer model: (a) temperature of the backfill and soil is constant, (b) temperature of the backfill and soil that is produced by circulating product through the pipeline for 16 h at a temperature that was initially constant and 9°F higher than the backfill and soil, (c) time history of the product temperature changes in the pipeline for the initial ground conditions shown in (a) and (b).

As shown in Figure 4.6, three sensors should be positioned in the ground somewhere near the midpoint of a 2-in.-diameter pipeline and located 2, 4, and 12 in. away from the outside edge of the pipeline. The most distant temperature sensor is intended to measure the ground temperature at a location that is not significantly influenced by the product in the pipeline. If the temperature sensors are too close to the dispensing end of the pipeline, their readings could be adversely influenced by ambient air temperature or convective mixing from product in the vertical extension of the pipe leading into the dispenser. It is therefore recommended that the sensor array be located at least 5 ft into the line from either the dispenser or the tank. This may not be possible at an operational UST facility that is being used as an instrumented test facility. If there are multiple pipes in the backfill, it is preferable to use only the outer pipe. The fourth sensor should be located in the tank, approximately 4 in. from the bottom (or in whatever container is used to store the product pumped into the pipeline during a test); this provides an estimate of the temperature of the product that is pumped from the tank into the pipeline.

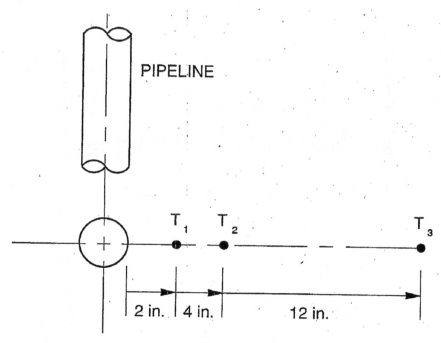

Figure 4.6. Geometry of the temperature measurements to be made in the backfill and soil surrounding an underground pipeline.

The temperature sensors should be calibrated before each evaluation, or more frequently, if required. Calibration is done by inserting the temperature sensors in a water bath that is continuously being mixed and simultaneously recording the output of these sensors and a reference sensor. The precision of the reference sensor should be 0.02°F. The accuracy of the reference sensor need only be good to the nearest 1°F. Calibration data should be obtained in increments of 5 to 10°F or less over the range of ground and product temperatures to be encountered during the evaluation; a calibration starting at 35°F and ending at 90°F would suffice. At least five points are required to complete the calibration. A calibration curve is generated by fitting a regression line to the temperature measured by each sensor being calibrated (y axis) and the temperature of the water bath from the reference sensor (x axis). The precision of each temperature sensor is estimated from the standard deviation of the ordinate (y axis). The accuracy of each temperature sensor is estimated from the intercept of the curve. It is not essential that the absolute accuracy of each sensor be known, but rather that each temperature sensor measure the same value. The relative accuracy is determined from the standard deviation of the intercepts of each calibration curve or from the standard deviation of a given temperature calculated from each calibration curve.

4.4.2 Measurement of Product and Ground Temperatures

The temperature conditions in the pipeline during a test must be characterized. The procedure used to characterize the temperature conditions varies slightly depending on the type of facility being used: a specialized test facility, one or more instrumented operational UST facilities, or several operational UST facilities that are not instrumented. When temperature conditions are generated at an instrumented test facility, product is taken from the bottom of the tank, pumped into the line, and circulated continuously there for one hour. This serves three purposes: (1) to produce a difference in temperature between the product in the pipeline and the surrounding backfill and soil, (2) to produce a temperature distribution in the surrounding backfill and soil that is similar to that produced by dispensing product at operational UST facilities, and (3) to produce repetitive temperature conditions from test to test. The end of the hour marks the start of a leak detection test or an initial waiting period. At an instrumented operational UST facility, a leak detection test should be initiated at the end of the day immediately after dispensing operations have ceased. The one-hour circulation period is then not required, since dispensing of product during normal business hours has the same effect on the temperature of the backfill and soil (and therefore on the rate of change of product temperature) as circulating the product does. Before a test is begun, however, the entire contents of the line must be flushed for 5 min with product from the bottom of the tank to produce the temperature condition. When five or more noninstrumented operational UST facilities are used, product is, as with the instrumented operational facility, already adequately mixed, and the test may begin after dispensing operations have ceased or at the close of the business day.

Model calculations suggest that the rate of change of temperature of the product in the pipeline depends on the distribution of the temperature of the backfill and soil immediately around the pipeline even though the difference in temperature between (a) the product in the pipeline and (b) the soil thermally undisturbed by the pipeline is the same. One could produce a temperature condition by circulating product through the pipeline for 5 min, and then start a test; however, to ensure repetitive conditions, one would have to wait 8 h after the test before producing another temperature condition.

The temperature condition for a particular test is calculated from the following formula

$$\Delta T = T_{TB} - T_G \qquad (4.3)$$

where

ΔT = difference between the temperature of the product at the bottom of the tank and a weighted average of the temperature of the ground surrounding the pipeline

T_{TB} = temperature of the product 4 in. from the bottom of the tank or the temperature of the product to be circulated through the pipeline

T_G = $[((T_1/3) + (2\,T_2/3))/3] + [2\,T_3/3]$ = weighted average of the temperature of the ground surrounding the pipeline

T_1, T_2, T_3 = temperature of the backfill or soil measured 2, 4, and 12 in. from the outer wall of the pipeline

This equation accounts for the insulating effect of the ground around the pipeline and the effect of the temperature of the undisturbed ground.

4.5 TRAPPED VAPOR

The pipeline used in the evaluation should be free of any trapped vapor. The sensitivity of the leak detection system to vapor can be assessed by trapping a known volume of vapor in the pipeline and conducting one or more leak detection tests. A simple device has been developed to do this.

4.5.1 Equipment and Instrumentation for Generating Trapped Vapor

Vapor can be trapped in a pipeline system by means of the vapor pocket apparatus shown in Figure 4.7. This apparatus can be constructed from common materials that can be purchased at any hardware store. The apparatus consists of a 1.5-in.-diameter tube that has a volume of approximately 100 ml; the device used in our experiments had a volume of 6.4 in.^{3} (105 ml). The tube is capped at the top and bottom and has two valves that can be opened and closed manually. The volume of vapor trapped in the line nominally depends on the length of the tube. Table 4.2 gives the volume of trapped vapor in the device as a function of pressure. The diameter of the tube can be other than 1.5 in. providing that the volume of the container at zero pressure is greater than 100 ml.

To measure the volume of the container we submerge the vapor pocket apparatus in water and then close both valves. After removing any excess water from the inlet or outlet tubes, we can measure the volume of the water in the container by emptying it into a graduated cylinder and taking a reading of the level to the nearest 1 ml.

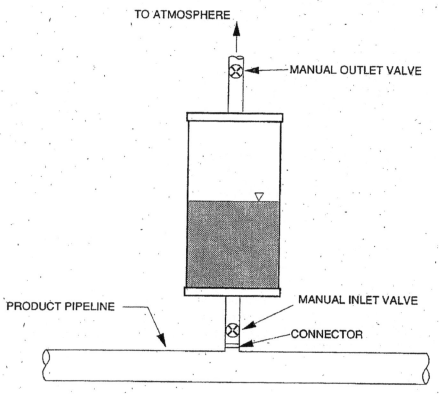

Figure 4.7. Mechanical device for trapping vapor in a pipeline system.

Table 4.2. Volume of Trapped Vapor in a Tube 1.5 in. in Diameter and 3.5 in. in Length as a Function of Pipeline Pressure

Line Pressure (psi)	Container Volume*	
	(ml)	(in.³)
0	105.2	6.42
5	78.5	4.79
10	62.6	3.82
15	52.1	3.18
20	44.6	2.72
25	38.9	2.38
30	34.6	2.11

* Assuming that atmospheric pressure is 14.7 psi.

To measure the volume of the container we submerge the vapor pocket apparatus in water and then close both valves. After removing any excess water from the inlet or outlet tubes, we can measure the volume of the water in the container by emptying it into a graduated cylinder and taking a reading of the level to the nearest 1 ml.

The entire vapor pocket apparatus must be air-tight. We can check this by spraying a solution of soapy water at all joints when the device is under pressure and looking for bubbles.

The vapor pocket apparatus can be attached to any part of the pipeline while both the inlet and outlet valves are closed. Once the apparatus is attached to the line, the outlet valve should be opened to release any residual air that may have been trapped. Then the outlet valve is closed and the inlet valve is opened to allow product from the pipeline to enter the container and pressurize it. When the inlet valve is open, a known volume of vapor is trapped in the line. The volume of trapped vapor will depend on line pressure. The vapor pocket apparatus should be insulated during the measurements.

4.5.2 Measurement of Trapped Vapor

The presence of trapped vapor in a pipeline can be identified from the pressure-volume data collected for estimating the bulk modulus of the pipeline system. As shown in Figure 3.1, the pressure-volume curve, which can be used to estimate B/V_o for the pipeline system, is linear in the absence of any vapor in the line. Curvature suggests the presence of trapped vapor. The volume at zero pressure is known. If the pressure-volume relationship for vapor is known, the volume of the trapped vapor in the device can be estimated. It is not necessary to calculate and report the volume of the trapped vapor if this device is used. The volume of vapor trapped in the device can be estimated from the following equation of state for a gas

$$p_1 V_1^n = p_2 V_2^n,$$
$$(4.4)$$

where p_1 and V_1 are the absolute pressure and volume of the vapor in the line at one pressure, p_2 and V_2 are the absolute pressure and volume of the vapor in the line at a second pressure, and n is the gas constant (assumed to be 1.0). Because of the discontinuity in the pressure-volume curve exhibited in the absence of any vapor (see Figure 3.1), this relationship cannot be easily used if a mechanical line leak detector is present in the line.

SECTION 5

SELECTION OF EVALUATION CONDITIONS

This protocol requires that the performance of the system be estimated under a wide range of temperature conditions and leak rates. Section 5 describes how to select the temperature of the product in the pipeline and the size of the leak in the line. The conditions selected for an evaluation should reflect the actual conditions under which the system will be used in the field.

5.1 TEMPERATURE CONDITIONS IN THE PIPELINE

All dispensing through a pipeline should be terminated during a leak detection test on that line. Dispensing through other pipelines buried in the same backfill and in close proximity to the pipeline being tested (i.e., within 12 in. of it) should also be terminated. This is because the temperature of the product in adjacent pipelines can affect the rate of change of the temperature in the pipeline being tested.

Table 5.1 summarizes the number of tests that must be done for each of the nominal conditions for which histograms must be generated. A nominal temperature condition is defined by Eq. (4.3) and requires that product from the tank be dispensed through the pipeline for 1 h or longer. It is assumed that the temperature conditions within the range of each 10°F increment will be as uniformly distributed as possible. This is particularly important for the conditions centered on 0°F; about half of the conditions should be positive and about half should be negative.

Table 5.1. Number of Tests Required for Each Range of Temperature Conditions

Number of Tests	Percentage of Tests	Range of ΔT (°F)
1	4	$\Delta T < -25$
4	16	$-25 \leq \Delta T < -15$
5	20	$-15 \leq \Delta T < -5$
5	20	$-5 \leq \Delta T < +5$
5	20	$+5 \leq \Delta T < +15$
4	16	$+15 \leq \Delta T < +25$
1	4	$\Delta T \geq +25$

*ΔT is the temperature difference between the ground and the product in the tank estimated from Eq. (4.3).

At an instrumented test facility, temperature conditions can be created by warming or cooling the product to be circulated through the pipeline. The following procedure should be used when multiple temperature conditions are generated during any one day. As a general rule, the temperature difference between the ground and the product circulated through the pipeline should change in only one direction. Figure 5.1 illustrates a set of three temperature conditions generated over the course of one day. The backfill and soil are initially at the

51

same temperature as the product added to the pipeline. Model calculations indicate that these same conditions can be regenerated on successive days providing that the ground is not subject to different ambient temperature effects. In the example in Figure 5.1, the test took 2 h. When accompanied by a 1-h circulation period, the minimum amount of time necessary to complete each test is 3 h. Three tests can be completed in a 9-h day. All of the tests for which temperature differences are positive should be done first. A period of 12 h or longer, during which no product is dispensed through the pipeline, should be allowed to elapse before the negative-temperature tests are begun. It is acceptable to increase the temperature of the product that is circulated through the pipeline in equal increments with respect to the initial temperature difference between this product and the ground 12 in. from the pipeline (i.e., T_3); however, the reported ΔT is calculated by means of Eq. (4.3) from the temperature measurements made before the circulation is started. Table 5.2 presents a testing protocol in which three temperature conditions are produced each day; for this example it is assumed that $T_3 = 60°F$. This test sequence is a good example of one that satisfies the general test matrix given in Table 5.1. Three vapor pocket tests, which satisfy the criteria presented in Section 3, are included at the end of Table 5.2. These tests, denoted by an asterisk, are included at the end of Table 5.1 to better illustrate this example of a temperature matrix. In an evaluation, the three trapped vapor tests should be randomly distributed in the test matrix. Assuming three to six tests per day, the temperature conditions can be generated by circulating product at the temperature given by T_{TB} and calculating ΔT from Eq. (4.3). The temperature conditions that result should satisfy the test matrix in Table 5.1.

The temperature conditions can be also be randomly generated, but it is important that the absolute value of the tank/ground temperature differences on any given day of testing always increase or always decrease. For example, any of the following three sets is acceptable: (1) -2.5, -5.0, -7.5°F, (2) +10.0, +12.5, +15.0°F, or (3) -2.5, -15.0, -20.0°F. On the following day a set of temperature conditions with a different sign can be used providing that at least 12 h have elapsed since the last test. It is not acceptable to both increase and decrease the temperature condition during the course of a single day (e.g., -2.5, +2.5, -5.0°F). A detailed procedure for randomly selecting temperature conditions so that they satisfy the above criteria is complex and unnecessary. If this is to be a blind test, the temperatures can be placed in any order providing that the above daily criteria are met.

If an instrumented operational UST facility (Option 2) is being used to evaluate the leak detection system, it is unlikely that more than one temperature condition can be generated on any one day. The temperature condition will depend on the product in the pipeline and the temperature of the ground. Unless there is a way to change the temperature of the product brought from the tank in to the pipeline, an evaluation performed at an operational facility will take significantly longer than one performed at a special test facility (Option 1). Enough tests must be conducted to satisfy the test matrix given in Table 5.1. The time required to collect these data can be reduced if more than one operational facility is used, particularly if the facilities have sufficient geographical separation to have different climates during a given season (e.g., Miami, Florida, and Chicago, Illinois, during the winter). With more than one instrumented operational UST facility, a larger range of

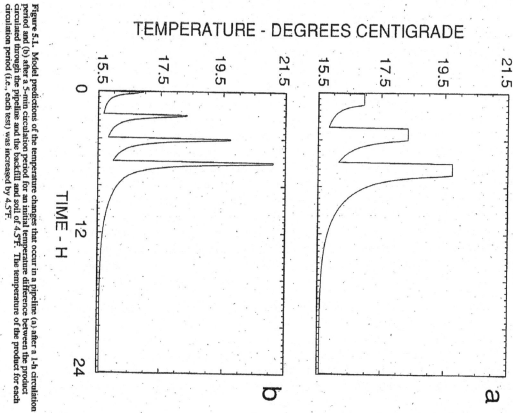

Figure 5.1. Model predictions of the temperature changes that occur in a pipeline (a) after a 1-h circulation period and (b) after a 5-min circulation period for an initial temperature difference between the product circulated through the pipeline and the backfill and soil of 4.5°F. The temperature of the product for each circulation period (i.e., each test) was increased by 4.5°F.

temperature conditions will be encountered over a shorter period of time. The total time required to complete this type of evaluation may be one to six months. Measurement of temperature is not required if Option 3 or 4 is chosen.

More than 25 tests may be needed in order to complete the test matrix of temperature conditions shown in Table 5.1. Unlike a special test facility, where temperature conditions can be controlled, operational facilities require more time for evaluators to gather the required number of tests. It is difficult to acquire exactly the specified number of tests in each temperature category. Inevitably some categories will contain a larger percentage of tests than others. For example, 20 tests rather than 5 may be conducted under the most benign condition, yet only one at each of the most extreme conditions, changing the relative percentage of tests in each of the seven categories in Table 5.1. This presents a problem because it produces a biased performance estimate. Assuming that performance declines as the temperature condition becomes more extreme, it is likely that the estimate of performance obtained from this 40-test sequence would be better than it would have been if the 25-test sequence in Table 5.1 had been followed exactly. Even if the total number of tests exceeds 25, there are still ways to avoid biasing the results. One is to randomly select test results in each category until the required number or percentage of tests is obtained. Similarly, the matrix can be based on the category with the largest percentage of tests if all the other categories are proportionally increased by means of a random selection within the category. The relative percentage of tests should be as it appears in Table 5.1. This means that in some categories the same test results may be used more than once. Either approach, then, avoids bias in test results in situations when more than 25 tests are needed to complete the test matrix given in Table 5.1. The latter approach has the advantage of using all the data. One might be tempted to try to avoid bias by using the first n results in each category, discarding any results obtained from tests beyond the required number; unfortunately this approach itself could bias the results if all the data from each category were obtained from one end of the category range.

There are many methods that can be used to randomly select the required number of test results from each category. One method is to used a random drawing procedure. One way of doing this is as follows: (1) assign a number to each test result in the category (1 through n); (2) write each number on a piece of folded paper and place these in a bowl; (3) blindly select pieces of paper from the bowl until the required number (or percentage) of tests for that category is obtained. A computerized version of this procedure could also be used.

Table 5.2. Recommended Procedure for Generating a Temperature Condition at an Instrumented Test Facility

Test Number	T_{TB} (°F)	T_3 (°F)	ΔT (°F)
1	60	60	0
2	62	60	2
3	64	60	4
4	66	60	6
5	68	60	8
6	70	60	10
7	72	60	12
8	74	60	14
9	77	60	17
10	79	60	19
11	81	60	21
12	83	60	23
13	86	60	26
Wait 12 h or longer before proceeding with test matrix			
14	58	60	-2
15	56	60	-4
16	54	60	-6
17	52	60	-8
18	50	60	-10
19	48	60	-12
20	46	60	-14
21	43	60	-17
22	41	60	-19
23	39	60	-21
24	37	60	-23
25	34	60	-26
26*	74	60	14
27*	74	60	14
28*	74	60	14

5.2 INDUCED LEAK RATES

It is desirable to perform, if possible, more than one leak detection test under each temperature condition, because this will reduce the amount of time necessary to complete an evaluation. If circumstances permit the generation of more than one temperature condition in a single day, the noise histogram can be generated from a test on a nonleaking line and the signal-plus-noise histogram can be generated from a test on a line leaking at the EPA-specified rate and possibly at other leak rates too. This is sometimes difficult to do, because the temperature of the product can change significantly from one measurement period to another, even though these measurements are closely spaced. Generally, the guidelines for closely spaced multiple leak detection tests at different leak rates under a given temperature condition, including a test on a tight line (i.e., a leak rate of 0.0 gal/h), are as follows:

- Up to *three* tests can be conducted if the leak detection system's test protocol requires a waiting period between the last input of product into the pipeline and the start of the data collection period, if this waiting period is greater than 6 h, and if the duration of the data collection period for each test is 1 h or less.

- Up to *three* leak detection tests can be conducted if the duration of the data collection period is less than 20 min, regardless of the length of the waiting period.

- Up to *two* leak detection tests can be conducted if the waiting period is greater than 4 h and the duration of the data collection period for each test is 1 h or less.

- Up to *two* leak detection tests can be conducted if the duration of the data collection period is less than 30 min, regardless of the duration of the length of the waiting period.

If multiple tests are conducted under the same temperature condition, the order of the leak rates should be randomly selected. This is important because the rate of change of temperature decreases with time and the test results would be biased if data for the same leak rate were always collected first. If one of these criteria for multiple tests cannot be satisfied, a new temperature condition must be created for each leak rate.

There are two types of testing scenarios: the test crew can have full knowledge of the conditions, or they can be placed in a blind testing situation.

5.2.1 Known Test Conditions

In the first scenario, the temperature and leak conditions are known by both the testing organization (the manufacturer of the leak detection system) and the evaluating organization. This scenario includes tests at a minimum of two leak rates, 0.0 gal/h and the EPA-specified leak (i.e., 0.1, 0.2, or 3.0 gal/h) for which the performance is to be determined. If the relationship between the signal-plus-noise provided by the manufacturer can be verified experimentally, it can be used to generate a signal-plus-noise histogram. (The way to do this is to shift the noise histogram appropriately.) It is then not necessary to conduct tests at the EPA-specified leak rate. The temperature conditions will be generated from smallest to largest, first for positive tank/ground temperature differences and then for negative. If the requirements for multiple testing are satisfied, the order of the leak rates for each test under a given temperature condition should alternate; there must be a total of 25 temperature conditions, satisfying the general range of conditions in Table 5.1. If the requirements for multiple tests are not satisfied, only one test can be done under each temperature condition, and the number of temperature conditions that must be generated doubles to a total of 50. Table 5.3 presents a set of suggested test conditions for two leak detection tests per temperature condition. Table 5.3 is based upon the temperature conditions in Table 5.2. Leak rates of 0.0 gal/h (required to generate the noise histogram) and 0.1 gal/h (required to generate the signal-plus-noise histogram for the line tightness test specified by the EPA regulation) are used. The three trapped vapor tests are also included at the end of the test matrix and are denoted by an asterisk. In an evaluation, these tests should be randomly distributed throughout the test matrix.

Table 5.3. Example of Test Conditions When More Than One Test Can Be Done for a Temperature Condition

Test Number	T_{TB} (°F)	T_s (°F)	ΔT (°F)	Leak No. 1 (gal/h)	Leak No. 2 (gal/h)
1	60	60	0	0.1	0
2	62	60	2	0	0.1
3	64	60	4	0.1	0
4	66	60	6	0.1	0
5	68	60	8	0.1	0
6	70	60	10	0	0.1
7	72	60	12	0.1	0
8	74	60	14	0	0.1
9	77	60	17	0.1	0
10	79	60	19	0	0.1
11	81	60	21	0	0.1
12	83	60	23	0	0.1
13	86	60	26	0.1	0
Wait 12 h or longer before proceeding with test matrix					
14	58	60	-2	0.1	0
15	56	60	-4	0	0.1
16	54	60	-6	0.1	0
17	52	60	-8	0.1	0
18	50	60	-10	0	0.1
19	48	60	-12	0	0.1
20	46	60	-14	0	0.1
21	43	60	-17	0.1	0
22	41	60	-19	0.1	0
23	39	60	-21	0.1	0
24	37	60	-23	0.1	0
25	34	60	-26	0	0.1
26*	74	60	14	0	0.1
27*	74	60	14	0	0.1
28*	74	60	14	0	0.1

5.2.2 Procedures for Blind Testing

Full-scale blind testing is not possible because the test crew knows, from this protocol, what leak rates are used in the evaluation and that the temperature conditions will be systematically increased or decreased. However, they do not know the order in which the leaks will be generated, and they do not know what temperature condition is being used; partially blind tests are therefore possible. There are two types, described below as Procedure 1 and Procedure 2. In Procedure 1 there are two leak rates, one of which will be zero and the other of which will be the EPA-specified leak rate. The same number of tests (usually 25) is conducted at each leak rate. Then there are three to five additional tests under unknown temperature conditions and at an unknown leak rate. In Procedure 2, there are four leak rates: 0, 0.05, 0.1, and 0.2 gal/h for monthly monitoring and line tightness tests and 0, 2.5, 3.0 and 3.5 gal/h for hourly tests. Twenty-five tests are conducted at the zero leak rate and 25 at either the 0.1 or 0.2 rate (the EPA-specified leak rates). Then an additional 13 tests are conducted at 0.1 or 0.2, and an additional 12 at 0.05. This brings the total number of tests to 75. In either procedure, as long as the test crew must report the results of one test before going on the next, blind testing will be assured. Any other procedure, or variation on the two procedures below, is acceptable if the same conditions for blind testing are met.

5.2.2.1 Procedure 1

Like the known-condition scenario, Procedure 1 requires that for each temperature condition at least 25 tests be conducted at a leak rate of 0.0 gal/h and at the EPA-specified leak rate. The difference between Procedure 1 and the known-condition scenario is that in the former the order of the leak rates per temperature condition is randomly selected, and between three and five additional temperature and leak conditions are introduced. These three to five additional tests, which will not be included in the performance analysis, will represent temperature differences greater than $\pm15°F$ between the tank and the ground, split as evenly as possible between positive and negative, and leak rates between 0.1 and 0.5 gal/h. In these extra tests, the nature of the temperature conditions, the size of the leaks, and even the number of tests are unknown to the test crew. The additional three to five tests tend to give large temperature- and leak-induced flow rates that might make the results look anomalous, and the test crew may be tempted to reject the results of such tests. However, if for any reason *other* than an obvious malfunction of the test equipment identified during the test itself the test crew declares one of these tests invalid, the evaluation should not be considered a blind test.

A random number generator or a random drawing of conditions can be used to select the number of extra tests, the leak rates, and the temperature conditions for each test. Or, the number of extra tests can be determined by writing the numbers 3, 4, and 5 on pieces of folded paper, placing these in a bowl, and randomly drawing one of the numbers. This can also be done by multiplying the output of a random number generator[*] (for example, a computer spreadsheet, scientific calculator or statistical tables) by five, rounding to the nearest integer value, and using the first number that is 3 or greater. Once the number of tests has been determined, a temperature condition must be selected for each test. If the number is odd, the extra temperature condition should be positive. Select one to three temperature conditions from the positive tank/ground temperature differences in the range +15 to +30°F, and randomly select one to three temperature conditions from the negative tank/ground temperature differences in the range -15 to -30°F. This can be done by randomly drawing

---

[*] It is assumed that any output of the random number generator is between 0.0 and 1.0.

temperature conditions, differing by increments of 1°F, from a container. This can also be done by multiplying the output of the random generator by 15, rounding to the nearest integer, and adding +15°F to get the positive temperature differences and subtracting -30°F to get the negative. Each leak rate in gallons per hour can be determined with a random number generator by dividing the output of the random number generator by 2.5 and adding the result to 0.1. Alternatively, twenty random selections of leak rates between 0.1 and 0.5 gal/h are given in Appendix D. Randomly select a number between 1 and 20 from a container to determine which table to use, and then select as many leak rates as there are tests to be conducted.

Acceptable methods of randomly selecting the leaks for the 25 tests under each temperature condition are as follows. If the criteria for conducting two tests under each temperature condition are met, the first and second leak rates for each temperature condition can be determined in the following way. Place two pieces of folded paper in a bowl, each piece of paper having one of the leak rates written on it, and randomly draw a number for each temperature condition; at least one of the leak rates for each temperature condition should be the EPA-specified leak rate. If a random number generator is used, its output for each leak can be rounded off to the nearest integer, with 0 being a leak rate of 0.0 gal/h and 1 being a leak rate equal to the EPA-specified leak rate. If the multiple-test conditions are not satisfied, a random drawing should be made for each temperature condition.

5.2.2.2 Procedure 2

Procedure 2 requires that for each of the 25 temperature conditions, the following tests be conducted: 25 leak detection tests at a leak rate of 0.0 gal/h; 25 leak detection tests at the EPA-specified leak rate, and 12 and 13 tests, respectively, at two other leak rates. Table 5.4 suggests the leak rates recommended for making an estimate of performance for the system at the EPA-specified leak rate.

Table 5.4. Recommended Leak Rates for Procedure 2

Number of Tests	Conditions for EPA-specified Leak Rates - gal/h		
	0.1	0.2	3.0
25	0.0	0.0	0.0
25	0.1	0.2	3.0
13	0.2	0.1	2.5
12	0.05	0.05	3.5

The first step in generating a matrix of leak conditions is to select the EPA-specified leak at which the leak detection system is to be evaluated. Each test run will use three out of four possible leak rates. These leak rates should be randomly selected for each temperature condition. A table of conditions can be generated as illustrated in Table 5.5. The leak rates for each test can be randomly selected by writing each of the four leak rates on a piece of paper, placing the folded pieces of paper in a container, and randomly drawing three leaks for each test. If a random number generator is used, assign a number between 1 and 4 to each of the four leak rates, multiply the output of the random number generator by 3, round to the nearest integer and add one to the integer. Three different numbers should be generated for each test.

Table 5.5. Illustration of a Possible Test Matrix for Evaluation of a Leak Detection System at 0.1 gal/h

Test No.	Temperature Condition ("F)	Leak Rate 1 (gal/h)	Leak Rate 2 (gal/h)	Leak Rate 3 (gal/h)
1	2.5	0.1	0.0	0.05
2	5.0	0.0	0.2	0.1
3	7.5	0.2	0.0	0.1
.	.	.	.	.
.	.	.	.	.
23	-20.0	0.0	0.1	0.2
24	-22.5	0.0	0.2	0.05
25	-25	0.2	0.1	0.0

Procedure 2 can be used to generate a performance estimate of the system at leak rates other than the EPA-specified leak rate. To do this, use the test results from the two alternative leak rates to generate a signal-plus-noise histogram. If the output of the leak detection system is reported, use the noise histogram, shifted by the difference between the mean of the noise histogram and the mean of each of the two alternative leak rates, to generate a signal-plus-noise histogram for each of these two leak rates. The signal-plus-noise histogram can be used directly for each of these two alternative leak rates if at least 25 tests have been conducted at each leak rate. To satisfy this test matrix, a total of 38 tests would have to be conducted to obtain 25 test results for each of the four leak rates. If the leak detection system does not output and report a measured quantity, but instead uses a preset threshold, a total of 25 tests is required for each leak rate at which a performance estimate is desired.

SECTION 6

EVALUATION PROCEDURE FOR SYSTEMS
THAT REPORT A FLOW RATE

Some leak detection systems measure an output quantity and compare it to a predetermined threshold to assess whether the pipeline is leaking. If the measured quantity is less than the threshold, the pipeline is declared tight. Otherwise, the pipeline is either declared leaking or another test is conducted to confirm or refute the results of the first. Other systems use a preset-threshold switch that is activated only if the changes in the line are large enough; no quantity is reported. The protocol for evaluating systems that measure and report the output quantity is described here in Section 6. The protocol for evaluating systems that use a preset-threshold switch is presented in Section 7. The procedure for evaluating both types of pipeline leak detection systems consists of the same general sequence of steps presented in Section 3.3. There are, however, slight differences in estimating the performance characteristics of the two types of systems and in how to analyze the noise and signal-plus-noise data to derive a performance estimate in terms of P_D and P_{FA}.

6.1 PERFORMANCE CHARACTERISTICS OF THE INSTRUMENTATION

Before performing any evaluation experiments with a leak detection system, it is necessary to ensure that the system is working correctly and is properly calibrated. An uncalibrated system could produce unexpected and sometimes meaningless results. In addition to this data quality assurance, the calibration also provides a measurement of the precision and accuracy (or bias) of the system's sensor(s). While these measurements may not necessarily be used quantitatively in the calculation of the P_D and P_{FA} of the system, they are used qualitatively to determine the advisability of proceeding with the evaluation. If the instrumentation (or system) noise is so large that the required performance could not be achieved even if no other noise sources were present, the evaluation procedure could be stopped, and a reassessment of the system design might be considered.

Each sensor used by the leak detection system should be calibrated in a controlled environment to determine what is being measured (i.e., specificity) and to make an estimate of the resolution, precision, accuracy, minimum detectable signal, and response time. For most instruments that measure a physical quantity (for example, volume, pressure, or temperature), the specificity is obvious. The resolution of the system is the smallest division for which a quantity is measured; since the resolution is usually well known, it does not have to be measured as part of this protocol, but it does have to be reported. The minimum detectable quantity is defined in this protocol as that quantity that can be detected with a P_D of 0.95 and a P_{FA} of 0.05; assuming that the instrumentation noise is normally distributed, the minimum detectable signal is 3.3 times larger than the precision.

An estimate of the precision and accuracy of each instrument should be made against a reference standard. This can be done by making three measurements of each of at least six different values of the measured quantity. These values should encompass the dynamic range of the system or the range of conditions under which it will be operated. The precision and accuracy are estimated from a regression line fit to the measured quantity plotted on the y axis and the reference standard plotted on the x axis. The precision is the standard deviation of the ordinate and the accuracy is equal to the intercept of the line. (See Appendix E for a description of how to calculate the mean and standard deviation of a set of measurements and how to fit a regression line to a set of measurements).

If a pressure transducer is used to monitor the pressure changes in the pipeline over a range of 0 to 40 psi, the calibration might be done at nominal intervals of 5 psi between 0 and 40 psi. Thus, three measurements would be taken at nine known pressures (e.g., 0, 5, 10, 15, 20, 25, 30, 35, and 40 psi). Performing the calibration exactly at 5-psi intervals is not essential. The calibration could be done at 1, 5.5, 9.7, 15, 21, 27, 31.5, 35.2, and 40.8 psi. It would also be acceptable to take data at six pressures in nominal intervals of 8 psi (e.g., 4, 12, 20, 28, 36, and 44).

An estimate of the threshold flow rate, defined at 20 psi, beyond which a leak will be declared is also required. For leak rates of 0.1 and 0.2 gal/h, the flow rate at which the threshold will be exceeded should be measured to within 0.015 and 0.030 gal/h, respectively; for a leak rate of 3.0 gal/h, the flow rate at which the threshold will be exceeded should be measured to within 0.25 gal/h. This estimate can be made on the pressurized pipeline system that will be used in the evaluation. (The sources of ambient noise, for example, the changes in product temperature, should be minimized while this estimate is being made.) Different leak rates are generated, from small to large, until the threshold is exceeded.

6.2 DEVELOPMENT OF THE NOISE AND THE SIGNAL-PLUS-NOISE DATA

In order to calculate the P_D and P_{FA}, one must first develop the cumulative frequency distributions (CFDs) from the histograms of the noise and the signal-plus-noise. As shown in Figure 2.4, the P_D and P_{FA} are derived from these CFDs along with the detection system's threshold and the leak rate of interest. In cases where the signal is independent and additive with the noise, the signal-plus-noise CFD is just a replica of the noise CFD shifted by the amount of the leak rate (as is the case in Figure 2.3). However, it cannot, in general, be assumed that the signal and the noise are linearly related. This relationship must be verified experimentally.

If the system uses a multiple-test strategy, the histogram of the noise and the histogram of the signal-plus-noise are generated from that test sequence which was the basis for declaring a leak. In addition to histograms used to develop a performance estimate of the system, a second performance estimate is requested. This second estimate is based only on the results of the first test in the multiple-test sequence. Refer to Section 3.2.3 for a discussion of multiple-test strategies.

In this protocol, it is assumed that the evaluation is being performed to obtain the P_D and P_{FA} at the leak rate specified in the EPA regulation for the type of system being evaluated, e.g., 0.1 gal/h for a line tightness test, 0.2 gal/h for a monthly monitoring test, and 3 gal/h for an hourly test. Thus, the procedure described below leads to the development of a noise CFD and a signal-plus-noise CFD for the leak rate of greatest regulatory interest for a line tightness test, a monthly monitoring test, and an hourly test. If local regulations specify leak rates more stringent than those in the EPA regulation, the local specification can be substituted for the EPA-specified leak rate.

Five options for developing the cumulative frequency distribution of the noise and the signal-plus-noise are described in the following sections. Each option is described in terms of procedure and data analysis. All require that the histograms be experimentally determined. The way to do this is to accumulate the results of tests that cover a wide range of temperature conditions.

6.3 EVALUATION PROCEDURE

The reader will recall, from Section 3.3, the general summary of the steps involved in the protocol. These steps are reiterated here, in a more specific way, as they apply to each of the five options. Step 2 of the protocol summarized in Section 3.3 presents the five options for collecting the data necessary to evaluate the performance of a pipeline leak detection system that measures and reports an output quantity. Since Step 2 is to choose one of the five options, which has obviously been done at this point, this step is omitted from procedures described below.

6.3.1 Option 1 - Collect Data at a Special Pipeline Test Facility

In Option 1, data are collected at special pipeline test facility. The histogram of the noise is generated from the results of actual tests with the leak detection system on a nonleaking pipeline over a wide range of environmental conditions. These conditions must include a wide range of product temperature changes. Option 1 is most easily implemented at a test facility like the EPA's UST Test Apparatus, where the integrity of the pipeline system is known and a range of environmental conditions can be generated and monitored quantitatively. The signal-plus-noise histogram for the EPA-specified leak rate can be compiled either directly from tests with the leak detection system over the same conditions used to generate the noise histogram or from the noise histogram and an experimentally validated relationship between the signal and the noise.

The test procedure will be applied to a pipeline system that meets the minimum specifications presented in Section 3.1. Below are the steps that should be followed to evaluate a leak detection system at a test facility. The steps correspond to those summarized in Section 3.3. Step 2, which is the selection of the evaluation option, has been omitted.

Step 1 - Describe the leak detection system to be evaluated. A general description of the leak detection system must be prepared before the system is evaluated. Attachment 1 in Appendix B is a form that is provided for this purpose; additional information can be included if so desired or if such information is necessary to complete the description of the system. The description includes the important features of the instrumentation, the test protocol, data analysis, and detection criterion. The system's test protocol should be followed during the conduct of the evaluation. If the system uses a multiple-test strategy to determine whether the pipeline is leaking or not, this same strategy should be followed during the evaluation.

Step 3 - Select leak rates and temperature conditions. Option 1 requires that 25 leak detection tests be conducted according to the system's testing protocol on a nonleaking pipeline under temperature conditions that satisfy the seven different categories of tank/ground temperature differences given in Table 5.1. Option 1 also requires that 25 leak detection tests be conducted under the same range of temperature conditions with a leak equal to the EPA-specified leak rate if a relationship between the signal and the noise is not known, or if a direct estimate of performance is desired at this leak rate. A matrix of temperature and leak conditions must be developed. The matrix depends on how the signal-plus-noise histogram is to be developed and whether the evaluation is to be done under conditions that are known or unknown to the test crew. A detailed description of how to generate a test matrix is presented in Section 5. Option 1 also requires that three tests be done with vapor trapped in the line. (The vapor pocket device described in Section 4.5 can be used to introduce the vapor into the line.) Thus, if this option is chosen, the minimum number of leak detection tests is 28.

Step 4 - Assemble the required equipment and diagnostic instrumentation. The following equipment and diagnostic instrumentation are required: leakmaker, pressure sensor, a minimum of four temperature sensors, pipeline compressibility device, vapor pocket device, graduated cylinders, and stopwatch. A description of the equipment and how to use it is presented in Section 4.

Step 5 - Verify that the line is not leaking. The pipeline system to be used in the evaluation has to be tight. Before the evaluation is begun, the line should be tested with a leak detection system that has a known performance. If a test facility is used, the integrity of the line does not have to be verified before each evaluation, but this should nevertheless be done at regular intervals. It is particularly important to verify that the pipeline system is not leaking if a third party evaluation is being performed. If there is a small leak in the pipeline, the performance of the system being evaluated will be unnecessarily degraded.

Step 6 - Measure the pipeline compressibility characteristics. The pipeline used in the evaluation should have a B of 25,000 psi; any system with a B between 15,000 and 40,000 psi is acceptable. Measurements of B/V_0 and B should be made when the temperature changes are small (i.e., less than 0.02°F over the duration of the measurement period) and should follow the procedure given in Section 4.3. The leak detection system should not be physically present in the line if it affects the magnitude of B or B/V_o. Unless temperature sensors such as thermistors are used to measure temperature in the line, measurements of B/V_o and B cannot be made until the pressure in the line stays within 1 psi over a period equal to the average duration of a B/V_o measurement (approximately 2 min). Three estimates of B and B/V_o will be made and the median value reported.

If the measured value of B is outside the specified range, the device described in Section 4.3 can be used to modify the compressibility characteristics of the pipeline and therefore the bulk modulus. Add the compressibility device to the pipeline and measure B/V_o. Repeat this procedure until B is as close to 25,000 psi as possible or is within the specified range.

The results of these measurements should be tabulated and reported on Attachment 3 in Appendix B.

Step 7 - Determine the performance characteristics of the instrumentation.
Estimates must be made of (1) the minimum quantity detectable by the system, (2) the precision and accuracy of each instrument used to collect the data over the dynamic range required for the measurements, and (3) the response time of the system. The resolution and flow rate of the threshold in gallons per hour must be reported. These measurements can be made in a special calibration unit or on the pipeline system itself when the noise is negligible. The general procedures required to estimate the performance characteristics of the instrumentation are described in Section 6.1.

Step 8 - Develop a relationship between the leak and the output of the measurement system, if necessary. If the relationship between the signal and the noise is known and a direct estimate of the signal-plus-noise histogram at the EPA-specified leak is not made experimentally, or if the general relationship between the signal and the noise is desired, the relationship must be verified experimentally. (This step is not necessary if the test matrix requires 25 tests at the EPA-specified leak rate.) The two-step procedure for developing this relationship is described in Section 4.2.3. The test results should be summarized in the tables in Attachment 7 in Appendix B. The appropriate forms from Attachments 4 and 5, which describe the temperature and leak conditions, as well as the test results, should also be completed.

Steps 9 and 10 - Collect the noise data, the signal-plus-noise data, and the trapped vapor data. The pipeline leak detector may have been isolated from the line during the bulk modulus measurements in Step 5. If so, it should now be reconnected so that the leak detection tests can be conducted. A leak detection test should be performed according to both manufacturer's protocol and the test matrix developed in Step 3. The result of each test should be recorded in terms of the output of the system. The three tests in which trapped vapor is present in the pipeline are also part of the test matrix and should be included in the overall data collection effort. There should be break of 12 h or longer between tests conducted under positive temperature conditions and those conducted under negative conditions. A temperature condition is created by circulating product through the pipeline system for 1 h before the test; the temperature of this product must be different from the temperature of the backfill and the ground around the pipeline. (The leak rate can be set at any time during this same 1-h period.) All dispensing through a pipeline should be terminated during a leak detection test on that line. Dispensing through other pipelines buried in the same backfill and in close proximity to the pipeline being tested (i.e., within 12 in. of it) should also be terminated.

The equipment and the procedures for generating a leak in the line are described in Section 4.2. If possible, all leaks will be generated at the at a line pressure equal to the pressures specified in Section 4.2 (i.e., 10 psi for hourly testing systems and 20 psi for all other types of systems). If this cannot be done, the leak can be generated at another pressure (e.g., the operating pressure of the line) provided that it is equivalent to leak rates defined in Section 4.2. The leak rate used in each test should be measured and reported. Once the leak has been generated, the line pressure can be readjusted, if this is required by the system's test protocol, to the appropriate pressure for the test.

The result of each test should be recorded in terms of the output of the system. These results constitute the data needed to build the histograms of the noise and the signal-plus-noise at the EPA-specified leak rate. If a multiple-testing procedure is used, noise and signal-plus-noise histograms must be compiled from the data used to determine whether the pipeline is leaking and from the first test of the multiple-test sequence; refer to Section 3.2.3 for additional details. The test results should be partitioned into the following groups:

(1) data from the 25 tests at a zero leak rate

(2) data from the 25 tests at the EPA-specified leak rate

(3) data from the tests at any other leak rate

(4) data from the three trapped vapor tests

(5) data from any extra tests

Compute the mean, standard deviation, and 95% confidence intervals on the means and standard deviations for the data in (1) through (3). The formulas necessary to perform these calculations are given in Appendix E.

The data in (1) are used to define the noise, and the data in (2) are used to define the signal-plus-noise at the EPA-specified leak rate. A performance estimate can be derived directly from cumulative frequency distributions of the noise and the signal-plus-noise according to the P_D/P_{FA} analysis presented in Section 6.4. Performance estimates can be made at the other leak rates from the noise data in (1) if the signal-plus-noise data in (3) are sufficient.

A signal-plus-noise cumulative frequency distribution can be generated for any leak rate if the relationship between the signal and the noise is known and has been validated experimentally with the data obtained in Step 6. The relationship between the signal and the noise is used to shift the noise histogram appropriately.

The temperature and leak conditions and the tests results obtained for these conditions should be tabulated and reported on Attachments 4 and 5 in Appendix B.

Step 11 - Sensitivity to Trapped Vapor. The results of the tests on lines with trapped vapor should be tabulated and reported on the standard form included as Attachment 6 in Appendix B.

Step 12 - Performance Analysis. The performance of the system can be calculated from the data partitioned for specific leak rates, $P_D s$ and $P_{FA} s$. The protocol is designed so that the P_D and P_{FA} of the system are established at the manufacturer's threshold and at the leak rate specified by the EPA regulation (i.e., 0.1, 0.2, or 3 gal/h) at a test pressure of 20 psi. If the evaluation is not done at the test pressure specified by the EPA, there is a method with which to calculate an equivalent leak rate at the non-EPA test pressure. So that each system can be compared to others, Attachment 2 in Appendix B provides tables for reporting a variety of performance estimates. If the leak detection system uses a multiple-test procedure, performance estimates should follow the system's protocol, and histograms should be generated from the data from both the last test and the first test. The analysis of the performance of a detection system in terms of P_D and P_{FA} is described in Section 6.4.

Step 13 - Evaluation Report. The results of the evaluation are tabulated and reported in the standard format presented in Appendix A and Appendix B. The performance characteristics of the instrumentation, the performance estimates of the system's ability to detect leaks under ambient environmental conditions, and the sensitivity of the system to trapped vapor will be presented in a standard set of tables. A leak detection system, as used in the field, meets the EPA standard for the leak rate specified in the regulation if the calculated P_D is 0.95 or greater and the P_{FA} is 0.05 or less. The temperature and leak rate conditions under which the system was evaluated should be tabulated and reported along with the test results for each temperature condition and each leak rate. The report also includes a general description of the pipeline system that was used in the evaluation. Finally, a section is provided for general comments.

6.3.2 Option 2 - Collect Data at One or More Instrumented Operational UST Facilities

In Option 2, data are collected at one or more instrumented, operational UST facilities. A special test facility (Option 1) has the equipment necessary to generate different temperature conditions. If this type of equipment is available at an instrumented operational UST facility, Option 2 is identical to Option 1. If there is no way to generate different temperature conditions, enough tests must be conducted to cover the range of temperatures specified in Table 5.1. The procedure for completing the test matrix so as to avoid biasing the performance estimate is described in Section 5.1. Other than this, the procedures are the same for both options.

6.3.3 Option 3 - Collect Data over a 6- to 12-month Period at 5 or More Operational UST Facilities

Option 3 is nearly identical to Option 2 except that the tests are conducted on a limited number of nonleaking, operational UST pipeline systems that represent the conditions under which the leak detection system will be used. In order to capture a range of climatic conditions, five different locations are used, each in a different region of the United States. In order to capture the seasonal effects at each location, periodic tests of the lines are conducted at intervals of approximately one month over a 6- to 12-month period. In Approach 3, at least 60 tests are needed (12 at each site, conducted at regular intervals). Because the stations are limited in number, the integrity of the pipeline systems should be verified, if possible, before the data collection begins. This option is best implemented when the relationship between the signal and the noise is well known. In this way, the signal-plus-noise histogram can be characterized without the need for extensive measurements at one or more of the sites. This option is particularly suited to automatic systems that routinely conduct a test of the pipeline whenever the UST facility closes.

Option 3 comprises the following steps, which correspond to those summarized in Section 3.3. Many of them are similar to those presented in Option 1. Again, Step 2 is omitted.

Step 1 - Describe the leak detection system to be evaluated. A general description of the leak detection system must be prepared before the system is evaluated. The form included as Attachment 1 in Appendix B is provided for this purpose; additional information can be included if so desired or if such information is necessary to complete the description of the system. The description includes the important features of the instrumentation, the test protocol, and detection criterion. The system's test protocol should be followed during the conduct of the evaluation. If the system uses a multiple-test strategy to determine whether the pipeline is leaking, this same strategy should be followed during the evaluation.

68

Step 3 - Select leak rates and temperature conditions. Option 3 requires that a minimum of 12 tests be conducted at each of the five operational UST facilities, for a total of at least 60 tests, over a 6- to 12-month period. The protocol requires that tests be conducted at intervals of approximately 2 to 4 weeks. They can be conducted more frequently if the evaluator so desires. A test must meet the following conditions:

- It must be started within 30 min of the last dispensing of product through the pipeline.
- It must be started within 12 h (preferably within 6 h) of a delivery of product to the tank.

Only stations that receive, on the average, a delivery of product to the storage tanks on a weekly basis can be used. Each test should be conducted as soon as possible after a delivery of product to the tank; this ensures that the temperature conditions will be approximately the same as those generated for Options 1 and 2. It is desirable to perform a leak detection test at each available opportunity (even as often as once per delivery). The date and time of the start and end of each test, the time that dispensing operations were terminated prior to the test, and the date and time of the last delivery of product to the tank should be recorded and tabulated. The nominal operating pressure of each pipeline system used in the evaluation should be measured and recorded. These data will be used to generate and interpret the noise histogram. Option 3 does not require that a set of tests be done at the EPA-specified leak rate and does not require that trapped vapor tests be conducted. It does require that the tests used in the performance analysis be conducted under the temperature conditions specified in Table 5.1. The geographical diversity of the stations and seasonal effects at each station will serve to satisfy those temperature conditions.

Step 4 - Assemble the required equipment and diagnostic instrumentation. The following equipment and diagnostic instrumentation are required: leakmaker, pressure sensor, graduated cylinders, and stopwatch. A description of the equipment and how to use it is presented in Section 4.

Step 5 - Verify that the line is not leaking. The pipeline used at each operational UST facility should be tight. Before the evaluation is begun, the line should be tested with a leak detection system that has a known performance. This protocol recommends that a tightness test be performed on each pipeline system, because if one or more of the pipelines is not tight, the performance of the system being evaluated will be unnecessarily degraded.

Step 6 - Measure the pipeline compressibility characteristics. The compressibility characteristics of the pipeline systems included in the evaluation should be measured and reported. There is no minimum specification to be met. Measurements of B/V_0 and B should be made when the temperature changes of the product in the line are small (i.e., less than 0.01°C over the duration of the

69

measurement period) and should follow the procedure given in Section 4.3. The leak detection system should not be physically present in the line if it affects the magnitude of B/V_o. Unless temperature sensors such as thermistors are used to measure temperature in the line, measurements of B/V_o and B cannot be made until the pressure in the line stays within 1 psi over a period equal to the average duration of a B/V_o measurement (i.e., approximately 2 min). Three estimates of B/V_o will be made and the median value reported.

If the pipeline leak detector was removed or isolated from the line during the compressibility tests, it should now be reconnected so that the leak detection tests can be conducted.

The results of these measurements should be tabulated and reported on Attachment 3 in Appendix B.

Step 7 - Determine the performance characteristics of the instrumentation.
Estimates must be made of (1) the minimum quantity detectable by the system, (2) the precision and accuracy of each instrument used to collect the data over the dynamic range of each instrument required for the measurements, and (3) the response time of the system. The resolution and flow rate of the threshold in gallons per hour must also be reported. These measurements can be made in a special calibration unit or on the pipeline system itself when the noise is negligible. The general procedures required to estimate the performance characteristics of the instrumentation are described in Section 6.1.

Step 8 - Develop a relationship between the leak and the output of the measurement system. In Option 3 it is impractical to develop a signal-plus-noise histogram at the EPA-specified leak using the *direct* approach. This histogram is generated instead from the relationship between the signal and the noise. This relationship must be verified by means of experiments at one of the operational UST facilities. The two-step procedure for checking this relationship is described in Section 4.2.3. The test results should be summarized in the tables in Attachment 7 in Appendix B. The appropriate forms from Attachments 4 and 5, which describe the temperature and leak conditions, as well as the test results, should also be completed.

Steps 9 and 10 - Collect the noise data, the signal-plus-noise data, and the trapped vapor data. Leak detection tests performed over a 6- to 12-month period at each site follow the guidelines established in Step 3. This data collection procedure will yield an estimate of the noise histogram that covers the temperature conditions under which the leak detection system will actually be used. All leak detection tests should be performed according to the manufacturer's protocol. The results of each test should be recorded in terms of the output of the system. All leak detection tests should begin immediately after dispensing operations have ceased. This is important because the rate of change of the temperature of the product in the pipeline decreases exponentially after the last dispensing of product. Dispensing through other pipelines buried in the same backfill and in close proximity to the pipeline being tested (i.e., within 12 in. of it) should also be terminated.

The results of these tests constitute the data needed to build the histograms of the noise and the signal-plus-noise at the EPA-specified leak rate. If a multiple-testing procedure is used, noise and signal-plus-noise histograms must be compiled from the data used to determine whether the pipeline is leaking and from the first test of the multiple-test sequence; refer to Section 3.2.3 for additional details. The test results should be partitioned into the following groups:

(1) for *all* pipeline systems and *all* operational UST facilities: tests that were started within *6 h* of a delivery and within 30 min of the last dispensing operation

(2) for *each* pipeline system at *each* operational UST facility: tests that were started within *6 h* of a delivery and within 30 min of the last dispensing operation

(3) for each operational UST facility where more than one pipeline system was used: tests that were started within *6 h* of a delivery and within 30 min of the last dispensing operation

(4) for *all* pipeline systems and *all* operational UST facilities: tests that were started within *12 h* of a delivery and within 30 min of the last dispensing operation

(5) for *each* pipeline system at *each* operational UST facility: tests that were started within *12 h* of a delivery and within 30 min of the last dispensing operation

(6) for each operational UST facility where more than one pipeline system was used: tests that were started within *12 h* of a delivery and within 30 min of the last dispensing operation

Compute the mean, standard deviation, and 95% confidence intervals on the means and standard deviations for the data in each of the data sets in (1) through (6). The formulas necessary to perform these calculations are given in Appendix E.

If at least two-thirds of the tests on each pipeline (i.e., at least 8 tests out of 12) were started within 6 h of a delivery, the data in (1) should be used to develop the noise histogram. Otherwise, the data from (4) should be used. The signal-plus-noise histogram at the EPA-specified leak rate is generated from the histogram and the relationship between the signal and the noise generated in Step 8. The relationship between the signal and noise is used to shift the noise histogram appropriately. A performance estimate is made from the P_D/P_{FA} analysis presented in Section 6.4. The leak rate is defined at a line pressure of 20 psi, and the performance estimate should

71

be presented in those terms. If more than 25 tests are available on any pipeline system in (2) or any operational UST facility in (3), additional performance estimates can be made. Estimates of performance can also be made as a function of time after delivery, after the last dispensing of product through the pipeline, or both, if data are available. Such an analysis, while not part of this protocol, can be useful in improving the performance of the leak detection system.

The temperature and leak conditions and the tests results obtained for these conditions should be tabulated and reported on Attachments 4 and 5 in Appendix B.

Step 12 - Performance Analysis. The performance of the system can be calculated from the data partitioned for specific leak rates, P_Ds and P_{FA}s. The protocol is designed so that the P_D and P_{FA} of the system are established at the manufacturer's threshold and at the leak rate specified by the EPA regulation (i.e., 0.1, 0.2, or 3 gal/h) at a test pressure of 20 psi. So that each system can be compared to others, a table for reporting a variety of other performance estimates is provided as Attachment 2 in Appendix B. If the leak detection system uses a multiple-test procedure, performance estimates should follow the system's protocol, and histograms should be generated from the data from both the last test and the first test. The analysis of the performance of a detection system in terms of P_D and P_{FA} is described in Section 6.4.

Step 13 - Evaluation Report. The results of the evaluation are tabulated and reported in the standard format presented in Appendix A and Appendix B. The performance characteristics of the instrumentation and the performance estimates of the system's ability to detect leaks under ambient environmental conditions will be presented in a standard set of tables. The report should indicate whether the performance estimate was made with data collected within 6 h or 12 h of a delivery of product. A leak detection system meets the EPA standard for the leak rate specified in the regulation if the calculated P_D is 0.95 or greater and the P_{FA} 0.05 or less. The data used in the evaluation should be tabulated and included as part of the evaluation report; this includes the date and time of the start and end of each test, the test results, the time of the last dispensing operation, and the date and time of the most recent delivery of product to the tank. In addition, a general description of the pipeline systems used in the evaluation should be presented, including the operating pressure and the bulk modulus of each pipeline system. Finally, a section is provided for general comments.

6.3.4 Option 4 - Collect Data over a 6- to 12-month Period at 10 or More Operational UST Facilities

Option 4 is like Option 3 in that testing is conducted on a large number of operational pipeline systems. It differs from Option 3 in that the integrity of the pipelines may not be known. Otherwise, the two are identical. Option 4 includes the same range of climatic conditions and requires the same number of tests per pipeline as Option 3.

Like Option 3, it is best implemented when the relationship between the signal and the noise is well known, and it is best suited to automatic systems that routinely conduct a test of the pipeline whenever the UST facility closes.

The histogram of the noise must be determined from analysis of the data. Since the status of the lines is not known, it is possible that some of the test results used to generate the histogram of the noise may be derived from lines with leaks. If *all* data are used in the analysis, the procedure developed for Option 3 can be followed directly. In some instances, it may be obvious that a line has a leak; those data can be removed for the analysis if field investigation supports this observation. However, removal of data from the analysis should be done with extreme care and should be clearly explained in the evaluation report. Removing data from the analysis is not justified, for example, simply because the test results from one pipeline (or a few test results from one or more pipelines) are significantly different from the majority of the test results. Any removal of data can bias the results, i.e., increase performance. Therefore, data should be removed only if it has actually been determined, through a special field test, that the line is leaking, or if it can be shown that anomalous results are due to instrumentation or equipment problems. In some cases, special data analysis strategies can be developed to statistically separate the test results derived from lines believed to be leaking from results derived from lines that are not leaking. The histogram of all the data and the histogram of the data actually used to develop the noise histogram should both be presented if any data have been removed. This approach will normally provide the largest database with which to make an evaluation but also requires the most care to characterize the histogram of the noise.

6.3.5 Option 5 - Develop the Noise and Signal-plus-noise Data from an Experimentally Validated Computer Simulation

In Option 5, models of the important sources of noise that control the performance of the leak detection system are developed and validated through a comprehensive set of experiments. These models are then used with models of the leak detection system to simulate the performance of the system over a wide range of conditions. The simulation results must then be checked experimentally. This check requires a set of tests with the actual leak detection system. In some cases, models of the noise cannot be developed with sufficient accuracy for the evaluation. In such a case, a database of measured conditions is collected and is used instead of the model. In general, Option 5 should be used with caution, because it is more difficult to implement properly than the other, more direct options for evaluating performance.

There are, however, a number of advantages to Option 5. First, this option is particularly useful if many systems of the same type are to be evaluated and compared, because each system will be tested under identical conditions. Second, with this option the performance estimates can be extended over a wider range of leak rates and pipeline configurations. Third, it is possible to limit the number of actual field tests with the leak detection system.

73

There are also a number of disadvantages to Option 5. First, it takes a significant technical effort to identify and develop simulation models of the sources of noise, and these models are necessary before any leak detection system can be evaluated. Second, accurate performance estimates require that all sources of noise that affect the particular leak detection system being evaluated be identified and included in the simulation. Third, accurate performance estimates require that each source of noise be properly modeled. Fourth, the operational practice, particularly the influence of the test operator, is usually not included in the evaluation, yet it may have a significant impact on performance. Fifth, for a number of reasons, it is easier to misuse Option 5 than it is the first four, especially because the evaluation conditions will ultimately become known and leak detection systems will be designed to perform well under these known conditions.

The disadvantages of computer simulation as an evaluation approach actually emphasize the strength of simulation as a design tool. Because tradeoffs in performance under a wide range of conditions can readily be examined, simulation is put to better use when it is applied to designing the specifications of a leak detection system rather than to evaluating its performance. Needless to say, if a simulation is used to develop a system, the same simulation should not also be used to evaluate it.

Option 5 can be used only when a leak detection system can be accurately described mathematically, when the models of the noise are validated experimentally, and when the simulation results are verified by means of experiments conducted with the actual system. Option 5 was the approach used to evaluate the performance of volumetric tank tightness test methods in the EPA program on that subject [7].

Only a general outline of the steps in Option 5 is provided below. This is because a different set of noise, signal-plus-noise, and leak detection system models would be required for each type of system to be evaluated. (For a description of the statistical topics discussed below, see Appendix E.)

Step 1. Develop a probability distribution, $P(N)$, for any noise source other than temperature that is applicable to the system being evaluated. (Temperature effects are included in Step 3 below.) The $P(N)$ may be derived empirically from the data or may be derived from a mathematical model that has been developed, validated experimentally, and exercised over a full range of conditions.

Step 2. Develop and validate experimentally a relationship between the signal and the noise.

Step 3. Develop a computer model of the leak detection system. The model should include:

- all quantities that are measured by the system

- the resolution, precision, accuracy, and dynamic range of the system's sensors

74

- any waiting periods that are included in the test protocol

- any deliveries and/or dispensing included in the test protocol

- the test duration as defined by the system's test protocol

- the data sampling rate

- the data analysis procedure

- the detection criterion

In addition, the output of the model must be in units of flow rate, and so conversion routines should be included in the model as needed.

Step 4. Develop the test simulation using

a) a heat-transfer model or a comprehensive set of field data to determine the rate of change of product temperature in the pipeline for a given set of ground and tank temperature conditions and a given set of dispensing conditions,

b) a model to estimate how the rate of change of product temperature affects any of the other noise sources and the output quantity being measured,

c) the relationship between height and volume in a given container to obtain the rate of change of volume for the noise sources defined in Step 1,

d) development of the signal-plus-noise probability distribution from Steps 2 and 4 (c), and

e) the leak detection system model developed in Step 2 in conjunction with pressure/volume/temperature relationships to determine the test outcome for a specified leak rate and the conditions described by Step 4 (a), (b), and (c)

Step 5. Validate the simulation with data obtained from a minimum of five actual leak detection tests on a nonleaking pipeline and five on a pipeline leaking at a known rate. The leak rate generated for the five leaking-pipeline tests should be equal to the leak rate at which the performance estimate will be made.

For all ten tests, the noise sources should be controlled, i.e., set to specific values which can then be used as input to the simulation. If all ten tests are within 15% of the results obtained by the simulation, the simulation is considered valid. The nominal temperature differences between the ground and the product dispensed through the pipeline system for an hour should be approximately -15, -7.5, 0, +7.5, and +15°F.

75

Step 6. Follow the steps in Option 1 to complete the evaluation, with one exception. Instead of conducting the field tests in Step 11 of Option 1, *use the simulation* to derive the data required to develop the noise and the signal-plus-noise histograms. The simulation should be exercised under the same conditions required by Option 1; all other field measurements, such as the measurement of the performance characteristics of the instrumentation, should be made in the same way as in Option 1. The tests required to estimate the sensitivity of the system to trapped vapor are usually done experimentally; they can be simulated if trapped vapor is one of the sources of noise included in the computer model.

6.4 CALCULATION OF P_D AND P_{FA}

The steps for calculating the P_{FA} and the P_D at a leak rate, LR, are given below, along with an example of how these calculations are done. These sample calculations are for tests conducted under the same temperature conditions on a nonleaking pipeline and for tests on a pipeline with a leak of 0.1 gal/h defined at 20 psi. The data collected on the nonleaking pipeline are used to generate a cumulative frequency distribution of the noise, and the data collected on the leaking pipeline are used to generate a cumulative frequency distribution of the signal-plus-noise. The same analysis procedure can be used if the cumulative frequency distribution of the signal-plus-noise is generated from an experimentally validated relationship between the signal and the noise and the cumulative frequency distribution of the noise. An example of how to estimate the probability of detection from this approach is also given. (See Tables 6.1 and 6.2.) In this example, it is assumed that the signal is independent of the noise and simply adds with the noise. The estimates of the P_{FA} and the P_D at a leak rate, LR, are for a specific threshold, T.

Estimating the probability of false alarm is done as follows.

1. Tabulate the available results of tests performed on a nonleaking pipeline, arranging them in order from the lowest value to the highest and numbering them sequentially (1 being the lowest).

2. Assign an individual frequency to each test result equal to $1/(n + 1)$, where n is the total number of test results.

3. Develop the cumulative frequency for each test result by multiplying the individual frequency of each result by the number assigned to each test in Step 1. The results are shown in Table 6.1. For example, the fifth test result would have a cumulative frequency of 0.192, which is equal to 5 times the individual frequency (i. e., $5/(n + 1)$), and a flow rate of -0.031 gal/h.

4. Generate a curve by plotting the test result on the abscissa (x axis) versus the cumulative frequency on the ordinate (y axis). This curve is the cumulative frequency distribution of the noise (the distribution of test results from nonleaking tanks), and corresponds to Figure 2.2.

76

Table 6.1. Values of the Cumulative Frequency Distribution of the Noise Shown in Figure 2.2

Cumulative Frequency	Test Result (gal/h)	Cumulative Frequency	Test Result (gal/h)
0.038	-0.092	0.538	0.000
0.077	-0.052	0.577	0.003
0.115	-0.042	0.615	0.008
0.154	-0.037	0.654	0.009
0.192	-0.031	0.692	0.014
0.231	-0.025	0.731	0.020
0.269	-0.015	0.769	0.022
0.308	-0.011	0.808	0.023
0.346	-0.010	0.846	0.027
0.385	-0.007	0.885	0.031
0.423	-0.005	0.923	0.042
0.462	-0.004	0.962	0.056
0.500	-0.002		

5. Locate the threshold on the abscissa of the curve generated in Step 4.

6. Estimate the P_{FA} from the intersection of the threshold and the cumulative distribution curve. This value is read from the ordinate at the intersection point. For a threshold of -0.05 gal/h, the P_{FA} equals 0.085 for the data plotted in Figure 2.4. This value can also be estimated by interpolation of the data in Table 6.1.

The P_{FA} can also be estimated from an analysis of how often the threshold was exceeded. The P_{FA} is calculated by dividing the number of times the threshold was exceeded by the total number of tests plus one. For the noise data in Table 6.1, $P_{FA} = 2/(25 + 1) = 0.077$.

Estimating the probability of detection at a specified leak rate (where the cumulative frequency distribution of the signal-plus-noise is generated from data collected on a pipeline with a specific leak) is done as follows.

1. Tabulate the available results of tests performed at the leak rate of interest, arranging them in order from the lowest value to the highest and numbering them sequentially (1 being the lowest).

2. Assign an individual frequency to each test result equal to $1/(n + 1)$, where n is the total number of test results.

3. Develop the cumulative frequency for each test result by multiplying the individual frequency of each result by the number assigned to each test (Step 1). The results are shown in Table 6.2. For example, the fifth test result would have a cumulative frequency of 0.192, which is equal to 5 times the individual frequency (i. e., $5/(n + 1)$), and a flow rate of -0.131 gal/h.

77

Table 6.2. Values of the Cumulative Frequency Distribution of the Signal-plus-noise Shown in Figure 2.3 Generated for Leak Rate (i.e., Signal) of 0.10 gal/h

Cumulative Frequency	Test Result (gal/h)	Cumulative Frequency	Test Result (gal/h)
0.038	-0.192	0.538	-0.100
0.077	-0.152	0.577	-0.097
0.115	-0.142	0.615	-0.092
0.154	-0.137	0.654	-0.091
0.192	-0.131	0.692	-0.086
0.231	-0.125	0.731	-0.080
0.269	-0.115	0.769	-0.078
0.308	-0.111	0.808	-0.077
0.346	-0.110	0.846	-0.073
0.385	-0.107	0.885	-0.069
0.423	-0.105	0.923	-0.058
0.462	-0.104	0.962	-0.044
0.500	-0.102		

4. Generate a curve by plotting the test result on the abscissa (x axis) versus the cumulative frequency on the ordinate (y axis). This curve is the cumulative frequency distribution of the signal-plus-noise (the distribution of test results from a pipeline with a leak of 0.1 gal/h). Negative values mean that product is flowing *out* of the tank or pipeline. This curve corresponds to Figure 2.3.

5. Locate the threshold on the abscissa of the curve generated in Step 4 under "Estimating the probability of false alarm."

6. Estimate the P_D from the intersection of the threshold and the cumulative frequency distribution curve. This value is read from the ordinate at the intersection point. For a threshold of -0.05 gal/h, the P_D equals 0.945 for the data plotted in Figure 2.4. This value can also be estimated by interpolation of the data in Table 6.1. Other estimates of P_D can be made against a particular leak rate by changing the threshold.

The P_D can also be estimated from an analysis of how often threshold was exceeded for a particular leak rate. The number of times the threshold was exceeded is divided by the total number of tests plus one. For the signal-plus-noise data in Table 6.2, $P_D = 24/(25+1) = 0.923$.

7. Other estimates of P_D can be made as a function of threshold and leak rate if the signal-plus-noise data have been collected for that leak rate or if the relationship between the signal and the noise can be developed from the existing cumulative frequency distributions. For each new leak rate (signal-plus-noise) curve, the effects on the P_D of changing the threshold can be estimated directly from the intersection of the threshold with the curve.

Estimating the probability of detection at a specified leak rate (where the cumulative frequency distribution of the signal-plus-noise is generated from the noise cumulative frequency distribution and an experimentally validated relationship between the signal and the noise) is done as follows.

1. Generate a cumulative frequency distribution of the signal-plus-noise for a specific leak rate, LR, by adding the system's response to the leak to each data point included in the cumulative frequency distribution of the noise using the manufacturer's relationship between the signal and the noise. If, for example, the signal is simply additive with the noise, the signal-plus-noise cumulative frequency distribution for an outflowing leak rate of 0.10 gal/h is obtained by adding -0.10 gal/h to each of the tabulated test results generated in Step 4 (i.e., in Table 6.1). This results in a shift of -0.10 gal/h in the cumulative frequency distribution of the noise.

2. Proceed with Steps 4 through 7 above.

SECTION 7

EVALUATION PROCEDURE FOR SYSTEMS
THAT USE A PRESET THRESHOLD

Some leak detection systems do not *report* the output quantity. Instead, they are designed to respond only if the output quantity is large enough to activate a preset-threshold switch. The procedure for evaluating preset-threshold systems differs only slightly from that for systems which report an output quantity. Many of the leak detection systems designed to meet the 3-gal/h hourly test requirement established in the EPA regulation use a preset threshold.

7.1 PERFORMANCE CHARACTERISTICS OF THE INSTRUMENTATION

Before performing any evaluation experiments with a preset-threshold leak detection system, it is necessary to ensure that the system is working correctly and will respond when the preset threshold is exceeded. This can be done with a simple calibration procedure. Depending on which option is selected, these measurements may or may not be used quantitatively in the calculation of the P_D and P_{FA} of the system, but they *are* used qualitatively to determine the advisability of proceeding with the evaluation. If the instrumentation (or system) noise is so large that the required performance could not be achieved even if no other noise sources were present, the evaluation procedure could be stopped, and a reassessment of the system design might be considered.

The calibration should consist of a sequence of measurements with the leak detection system in a controlled environment to determine what the system is measuring (i.e., specificity) and to make an estimate of the resolution, precision, accuracy, and minimum detectable signal. Preset-threshold systems, like those that report a flow rate, do measure a physical quantity, which is what triggers the threshold switch. The difference is that this quantity is not reported. For most systems that measure a physical quantity (for example, volume or pressure), the specificity is obvious. The resolution of the system is the smallest division for which a quantity is measured; since the resolution is usually well known, it does not have to be measured as part of this protocol, but it does have to be reported. The minimum detectable quantity is defined in this protocol as that quantity that can be detected with a P_D of 0.95 and a P_{FA} of 0.05; assuming that the instrumentation noise is normally distributed, the minimum detectable signal is 3.3 times larger than the precision.

The flow rate at which the threshold of the measurement system is exceeded, as well as the precision and accuracy of system, can be determined from the tests described below. These tests should be done on a pipeline system in which the temperature changes are negligible. The procedure is as follows:

- *Determine the threshold.* An estimate of the flow rate at which the threshold will be exceeded and at which the system will signal the presence of a leak is required. This flow rate is defined at a pressure of either 10 psi (for 3-gal/h hourly testing systems) or 20 psi (for all other systems). For leak rates of 0.1 gal/h (for a line tightness test) and 0.2 gal/h (for a monthly monitoring test), the flow rate at which the threshold will be exceeded should be measured to within 0.015 and 0.030 gal/h, respectively; for a leak rate of 3.0 gal/h (for an hourly test), the flow rate at which the threshold will be exceeded should be measured to within 0.25 gal/h. The sources of ambient noise in the pressurized pipeline system that will be used in the evaluation should be minimized. Different leak rates are generated, from small to large, until the threshold is exceeded.

- *Determine the minimum detectable signal.* The minimum detectable signal is less than or equal to the threshold.

- *Determine the precision.* The leak rate at which the threshold is exceeded is found by repeating the leak detection test a number of times, with the difference in the size of each leak rate getting progressively smaller until the system responds. The precision of the system is determined from the standard deviation of the five flow rates at which the threshold was exceeded is the precision of the system. The uncertainty of the precision estimate made with this method is dependent on the size of the increment between leak rates; as fine an increment as possible should be used.

- *Determining the accuracy.* The accuracy of the system is determined from the mean of the five flow rates used to estimate precision. The accuracy is the difference between the measured flow rate and the flow rate at which the manufacturer claimed that the system would respond. If no claim is made, an accuracy measurement cannot be calculated or reported.

7.2 DEVELOPMENT OF THE NOISE AND THE SIGNAL-PLUS-NOISE DATA

In this protocol, it is assumed that the evaluation is being performed to obtain the P_D and P_{FA} at the leak rate specified in the EPA regulation for the type of system being evaluated, e.g., 0.1 gal/h for a line tightness test, 0.2 gal/h for a monthly monitoring test, or 3 gal/h for an hourly test. Thus, the procedure described below leads to the development of the noise and the signal-plus-noise data for the leak rate of greatest regulatory interest for a line tightness test, a monthly monitoring test, and an hourly test. If local regulations specify leak rates more stringent than those in the EPA regulation, the local standard can be substituted for the EPA-specified leak rates.

Unlike those leak detection systems that quantitatively measure and report the output of the system, the only output from a preset-threshold system is a simple pass or fail[*] -- i.e.,

---

[*] Pass means that the threshold was not exceeded and fail means that the threshold was exceeded.

whether or not the system responded to the leak or the temperature condition. As a consequence, this is the only performance estimate that can be derived from the evaluation. It is not possible to examine the tradeoffs in performance by changing the threshold. An advantage of preset-threshold systems is that the analysis used to estimate P_{FA} and the P_D for the EPA-specified leak rate is simpler than it is for the systems that quantitatively measure the output; however, the latter can be analyzed the same way as the preset-threshold systems. The method of analysis is described in Section 7.4.

If the system uses a multiple-test strategy, the histogram of the noise and the histogram of the signal-plus-noise are generated from that test sequence which was the basis for declaring a leak. In addition to histograms used to develop a performance estimate of the system, a second performance estimate is requested. This second estimate is based only on the results of the first test in the multiple-test sequence. Refer to Section 3.2.3 for a discussion of multiple-test strategies.

7.3 EVALUATION PROCEDURE

The same five options for estimating the performance of the leak detection systems that report an output quantity are used to collect the data necessary to characterize the noise and the signal-plus-noise for systems that use a preset threshold. These options are presented in Section 6.3 and are not repeated here. There are only a few minor differences. First, the performance characteristics are determined according to the procedures presented in Section 7.1 and not Section 6.1. Second, the analysis required to estimate of performance in terms of P_D and P_{FA} follows the procedures presented in Section 7.4 and not Section 6.4. Third, the noise and the signal-plus-noise histograms must be measured directly.

Some systems that us a preset-threshold switch and are intended to meet the 3-gal/h hourly test requirements are designed to do a quick test of the pipeline system. Normally, the duration of a test ranges from a few seconds to tens of seconds because the system is designed to test the line at least once per hour between occurrences of product dispensing. Whereas most other systems have a test duration equal to the data collection time (i.e., the data that will be used in calculating a flow rate that will be compared to a threshold), the systems in question have a test duration equal to the difference between the time a system is activated and the time it responds to a leak. In these systems, the test duration may not be specifically defined, since the system does not control the response time. To avoid misleading or ambiguous results with these systems, therefore, the evaluator should ensure that the test duration is clearly defined in the manufacturer's test protocol. For the purposes of the evaluation, a test duration must be specified. The duration should be consistent with the normal operational practice and the manufacturer's intended use of the system. If it is not, the evaluator should clearly point this out in the report, for it may mean that the system being evaluated is not the same as the system being sold commercially in the sense that the system may not respond as quickly as (i.e., may have a longer test duration than) the user expects.

7.4 CALCULATION OF P_D AND P_{FA}

The performance analysis is done as follows. The P_{FA} is determined directly from the number of times the threshold was exceeded (the number of times the pipeline failed the test) in the zero-leak-rate data (the noise data) divided by the total number of tests plus one. Estimates of P_D can be made directly from the tests conducted at the EPA-specified leak rate and any other leak rate for which adequate data are available (i.e., 25 tests over the full range of temperature conditions). The P_D is the number of times the threshold was exceeded divided by the total number of tests plus one. The analysis is a simple tabulation. The data in Tables 7.1 and 7.2 are the same data found in Tables 6.1 and 6.2, but they are reproduced as if they had been collected with a preset-threshold leak detection system instead of one that reports an output quantity.

Table 7.1. Values of the Cumulative Frequency Distribution of the Noise Shown in Figure 2.2

Cumulative Frequency	Test Result (gal/h)	Cumulative Frequency	Test Result (gal/h)
0.038	Fail	0.538	Pass
0.077	Fail	0.577	Pass
0.115	Pass	0.615	Pass
0.154	Pass	0.654	Pass
0.192	Pass	0.692	Pass
0.231	Pass	0.731	Pass
0.269	Pass	0.769	Pass
0.308	Pass	0.808	Pass
0.346	Pass	0.846	Pass
0.385	Pass	0.885	Pass
0.423	Pass	0.923	Pass
0.462	Pass	0.962	Pass
0.500	Pass		

Table 7.2. Values of the Cumulative Frequency Distribution of the Signal-plus-noise Shown in Figure 2.3 Generated for Leak Rate (i.e.. Signal) of 0.10 gal/h

Cumulative Frequency	Test Result (gal/h)	Cumulative Frequency	Test Result (gal/h)
0.038	Fail	0.538	Fail
0.077	Fail	0.577	Fail
0.115	Fail	0.615	Fail
0.154	Fail	0.654	Fail
0.192	Fail	0.692	Fail
0.231	Fail	0.731	Fail
0.269	Fail	0.769	Fail
0.308	Fail	0.808	Fail
0.346	Fail	0.846	Fail
0.385	Fail	0.885	Fail
0.423	Fail	0.923	Fail
0.462	Fail	0.962	Pass
0.500	Fail		

The test results given in Tables 7.1 and 7.2 are derived from a system having a threshold switch set to -0.05 gal/h and subject to the same conditions as the system that reports an output quantity (see Tables 6.1 and 6.2). When the probability of false alarm is calculated from the test results in Table 7.1, $P_{FA} = 2/(25+1) = 0.077$. When the probability of detection against a leak rate of 0.1 gal/h is calculated from the test results in Table 7.2, P_D = 24/(25+1) = 0.923. (It should be noted that in an actual test, the data will not already have been sorted as has been done for the data in Tables 7.1 and 7.2.)

98

SECTION 8

LEAK DETECTION TESTS WITH TRAPPED VAPOR IN THE PIPELINE

If Option 1, 2, or 5 is used to characterize the noise and signal-plus-noise histograms, a special set of three tests will be conducted with a small volume of vapor trapped in the pipeline. These tests are intended to determine the sensitivity of the leak detection system to any residual vapor that might be trapped in a line during a test. The results of these three tests will be tabulated and reported, but will not be included in the histogram of the noise or signal-plus-noise used to estimate the performance of the system. Trapped vapor tests are not required in Options 3 and 4 because these options both require many tests at a large number of operational UST facilities; as a result, it is likely that trapped vapor will be present during some of the tests and that it will thus be included in the actual performance estimates.

If the system is being evaluated as a line tightness test or a monthly monitoring test, the three tests will be conducted with leaks of 0.0, 0.1, and 0.2 gal/h, and with vapor trapped in the pipeline. The amount of trapped vapor will be that produced by a 6.4-in.^{3} $\pm$ 0.6 in.^{3} (105-ml $\pm$10 ml) vapor pocket apparatus. These tests should be done under the same nominal temperature condition. If these are blind tests, the tests will be randomly mixed in with the other tests in the test matrix used to develop the noise and the signal-plus-noise histograms. If the system is being evaluated as an hourly test, the leaks generated for the three tests should be 0, 2.75, and 3.25 gal/h, respectively. If these are blind tests, the leaks should be in random order.

The vapor pocket apparatus shown in Figure 4.7 on page 49, which has been specially designed for this protocol, can be used to trap vapor in the pipeline. Trapped vapor is introduced in the line by opening or closing an inlet valve. Section 4.5.1) describes the apparatus and how it can be used to generate a vapor pocket.

The results of these three tests will be reported in Attachment 6 in Appendix B.

SECTION 9

REPORTING OF RESULTS

A form on which to summarize the results of the evaluation has been provided in
Appendix A. The form requires that the following information be provided:

- the name of the leak detection system that was evaluated and the name and address of
  its manufacturer

- the performance of the system for detection of a leak equal to the one specified in the
  EPA regulation in terms of probability of detection and probability of false alarm

- the criterion for declaring a leak, including (1) whether the system is one that reports
  the output and compares it to a threshold or whether it is one that uses a preset
  threshold, (2) the flow rate of a leak represented by the threshold, and (3) whether the
  system uses a multiple-test strategy

- the option used to collect the data for the evaluation

- a brief description of the pipeline system(s) used in the evaluation

- a summary of the range of temperature conditions used in the evaluation

- a summary of the leak rates used to make the performance estimate

- a summary of the sensitivity of the system to the presence of trapped vapor in the
  pipeline

- the performance characteristics of the instrumentation that comprises the leak detection
  system

- a brief description of the types of pipeline systems to which the leak detection system
  is applicable

- the important features of the protocol for conducting a test with this leak detection
  system

- a list of attachments to the form

- the name, address and telephone number of the organization that conducted the
  evaluation and the name, date, and signature of the individual who certifies that the
  system was evaluated according to the procedures outlined by the EPA

There are seven attachments to the form that give additional details about the system and the evaluation. With the data and information provided in these attachments, all of the results of the evaluation could be independently reviewed and verified. The seven attachments include:

- Attachment 1 - Description of the System Evaluated

- Attachment 2 - Summary of the Performance of the System Evaluated

- Attachment 3 - Summary of the Configuration of the Pipeline System(s) Used in the Evaluation

- Attachment 4 - Data Sheet Summarizing the Product Temperature Conditions Used in the Evaluation

- Attachment 5 - Data Sheet Summarizing the Test Results and the Leak Rates Used in the Evaluation

- Attachment 6 - Data Sheet Summarizing the Test Results and the Trapped Vapor Tests

- Attachment 7 - Data Sheet Summarizing the Test Results Used to Check the Relationship Supplied by the Manufacturer for Combining the Signal and the Noise

SECTION 10

TECHNICAL BASIS FOR VALUES USED IN THE PROTOCOL

The technical basis for the choice and number of test conditions is discussed below.

10.1 RANGE OF TEMPERATURE CONDITIONS

The range of temperature conditions generated for an evaluation is based on a study completed for the EPA [6,7]. The study estimated the average monthly difference in temperature between the air and the product in the tank. It can be assumed that the average air temperature is approximately equal to the temperature of the ground to a depth of 1 to 3 ft. The temperature of the product brought into the pipeline was estimated from empirical measurements made in underground storage tanks. Data from 77 cities throughout the United States were used to generate a histogram of these average differences. These data were collected during the two months that had the coldest and hottest average temperatures, i.e., January and July, respectively. The shapes of the histograms were nearly identical, i.e., the standard deviations were approximately equal, but the means were different. The study indicated that the mean temperature differences during January and July were -27°F (-15°C) and +9°F (+5°C), respectively. The standard deviation of the temperature differences for each month was approximately 9°F. If it is assumed that there is a similar distribution for each of the two months and a mean that is uniformly distributed between the minimum and maximum values determined by the January and July means, the temperature is approximately normally distributed. The temperature conditions selected for this protocol and shown in Table 5.1 are based on this analysis.

10.2 NUMBER OF TESTS

The number of independent tests required to evaluate the performance of a pipeline leak detector depends on the statistical uncertainty desired for the P_D and P_{FA}. Independence means that the individual tests are not correlated with each other. A high degree of correlation is found if the testing errors are systematic rather than random. When this is the case, the same error occurs in each individual test and the averaging effect, which can reduce the noise fluctuations, is not realized. If the tests are not independent, a larger number of tests is required if the same uncertainty is to be maintained. Most pipeline testing errors tend to be systematic, and a high degree of correlation is generally found, as, for example, when successive tests are conducted over a short time during which there are no temperature changes in the line, or when trapped vapor is present during each test. Since changes in the temperature of the product are the largest source of error in a vapor-free pipeline system, independence will be achieved if a different temperature condition is created for each test. A new temperature condition can be generated by pumping in product whose temperature is different from that of the product in the pipeline and that of the surrounding ground. At a test facility, a full range of temperature conditions can be created over a short period of time (two to four weeks) if the product can be heated or cooled before it is transferred to the line. If the tests are done at an operational UST facility, a new temperature condition is created each time there is a new delivery of product to the tank system. However, consecutive deliveries do not necessarily produce independent temperature conditions, because over a period of several weeks the temperature of the product delivered to the tank system and that of the ground surrounding the system tend to be similar. To guarantee a wide range of temperature conditions, data must be collected over a 6- to 12-month period. In order to avoid biasing the performance toward either the high or low end of the scale, the data from the UST facilities must be partitioned into groups according to the number of hours that have elapsed after a product delivery.

An estimate of the number of independent tests was made; it was assumed that the 95% lower and upper confidence intervals on the P_D and P_{FA}, respectively, gave a P_D no lower than 0.90 and a P_{FA} no higher than 0.10. This means that there is a probability of 95% that an instrument that has a P_D of 0.95 and a P_{FA} of 0.05 would have experimental P_D/P_{FA} values greater than 0.90 and 0.10, respectively. The estimate assumes that the cumulative frequency distribution (CFD) of the noise and the signal-plus-noise are normally distributed and that a threshold consistent with a P_{FA} of 0.05, the EPA minimum requirement, is used. It is further assumed that the signal is independent and additive with the noise. This means that the signal-plus-noise CFD is simply a shifted replica of the noise, i.e., the mean is equal to the signal and the standard deviation is the same. For this performance model, the P_{FA} and P_D can be determined from the standard deviation of the noise and signal-plus-noise CFDs. If it is assumed that the mean of the noise CFD is zero (i.e., that it has no bias), the 95% confidence interval on the standard deviation of the histograms is determined by the χ^2 (chi-squared) probability distribution. The 95% confidence intervals are determined by the number of independent tests. The uncertainty is large if the number of tests is small; the uncertainty decreases as the number of tests increases.

If the normal probability density performance model is used, the leak rate that can be detected with a P_D of 0.95 and a P_{FA} of 0.05 is equal to 3.28 standard deviations, and the threshold is equal to 1.64 standard deviations. If the leak rate is 0.1 gal/h, the standard deviation must be 0.03 gal/h; if the leak rate is 0.2 gal/h, the standard deviation must be 0.06 gal/h. The corresponding thresholds are 0.05 and 0.10 gal/h, respectively. If these thresholds are used, standard deviations of 0.039 for the 0.1-gal/h leak rate and 0.078 gal/h for the 0.2-gal/h leak rate would result in a P_{FA} of 0.10 and a P_D of 0.90. Thus, the upper 95% confidence interval on a P_{FA} of 0.05 and the lower 95% confidence interval on a P_D of 0.95 would result in the detection of leak rates of 0.128 and 0.258 gal/h, respectively, for the two leak rates of interest. These calculations suggest that a minimum of 32 tests is required.

It was decided to select 25 as the minimum number of independent tests required for the evaluation. (Statistically, the difference between 32 and 25 is very small.) The value of the standard deviation, the minimum detectable leak rate, and the P_D and P_{FA} for 25 independent tests defined by the 95% confidence intervals are summarized in Tables 10.1 through 10.3 for the detection of leaks of 0.1, 0.2, and 3.0 gal/h with a P_D of 0.95 and a P_{FA} of

0.05. These confidence intervals suggest the degree of uncertainty in estimating performance with 25 tests. Any experimental leak rate value determined from a 25-test evaluation that falls within the 95% confidence intervals on the minimum detectable leak rates given in Tables 10.1 through 10.3 for a P_D of 0.95 and a 0.05, or any P_D and P_{FA} that falls within the 95% confidence intervals of the P_Ds and P_{FA}s given in Tables 10.1 through 10.3, is not statistically distinguishable from the 0.1-, 0.2-, and 3.0-gal/h EPA standards.

Table 10.1. Experimental Uncertainty on the Standard Deviation of the Noise and Signal-plus-noise Histograms, the Smallest Leak Rates That Can Be Detected with a P_D of 0.95 and a P_{FA} of 0.05, and the P_D and P_{FA} Characterized by the 95% Confidence Intervals on the Standard Deviation for Detection of a Leak Rate of 0.10 gal/h

Quantity	Lower Confidence Interval	Mean	Upper Confidence Interval
Standard Deviation - gal/h	0.025	0.03	0.041
Smallest Detectable Leak Rate - gal/h	0.083	0.10	0.134
P_D	0.890	0.95	0.976
P_{FA}	0.024	0.05	0.110

Table 10.2. Experimental Uncertainty on the Standard Deviation of the Noise and Signal-plus-noise Histograms, the Smallest Leak Rates That Can Be Detected with a P_D of 0.95 and a P_{FA} of 0.05, and the P_D and P_{FA} Characterized by the 95% Confidence Intervals on the Standard Deviation for Detection of a Leak of 0.20 gal/h

Quantity	Lower Confidence Interval	Mean	Upper Confidence Interval
Standard Deviation - gal/h	0.050	0.06	0.0815
Smallest Detectable Leak Rate - gal/h	0.166	0.20	0.268
P_D	0.890	0.95	0.976
P_{FA}	0.024	0.05	0.110

Table 10.3. Experimental Uncertainty on the Standard Deviation of the Noise and Signal-plus-noise Histograms, the Smallest Leak Rates That Can Be Detected with a P_D of 0.95 and a P_{FA} of 0.05, and the P_D and P_{FA} Characterized by the 95% Confidence Intervals on the Standard Deviation for Detection of a Leak of 3.0 gal/h

Quantity	Lower Confidence Interval	Mean	Upper Confidence Interval
Standard Deviation - gal/h	0.76	0.91	1.22
Smallest Detectable Leak Rate - gal/h	2.5	3.0	4.0
P_D	0.890	0.95	0.976
P_{FA}	0.024	0.05	0.110

10.3 RANGE OF THE BULK MODULUS

The range of the bulk modulus (elasticity) is not well known for the population of underground storage tank pipeline systems found throughout the United States. Only several values of B have been measured. The value of B used in this protocol is based on a limited set of data collected during a program conducted for the American Petroleum Institute [4,5].

10.4 VAPOR POCKETS

Vapor trapped in the line can affect the performance of a leak detection system. There are two effects. First, the trapped vapor changes the bulk modulus of the pipeline system. This affects the magnitude of the conversion factor needed, for example, to convert a pressure measurement to a flow rate. Second, if there is a large amount of trapped vapor, thermally induced volume changes can affect the performance of the system because volume changes also affect pressure changes in the line. Some systems are particularly sensitive to the presence of trapped vapor and others are not. According to the evaluation protocol, the pipeline system should be as free of trapped vapor as possible. Thus, in general, the effects of trapped vapor will not be included in the performance estimates. If the effects of trapped vapor were included, the number of test conditions would have to be increased significantly. Because trapped vapor can have a measurable impact on performance, however, several tests must be done so that the sensitivity of the system to trapped vapor can be determined.

REFERENCES

1. U.S. Environmental Protection Agency, Underground Storage Tanks; Technical Requirements, 40 CFR Part 280, *Federal Register*, Vol. 53, No. 185 (23 September 1988).

2. United States Environmental Protection Agency, Standard Test Procedures for Evaluating Leak Detection Methods: Liquid-phase Out-of-tank Product Detectors, EPA Contract No. 68-03-3409, Work Assignment 02 (March 1990).

3. United States Environmental Protection Agency, Standard Test Procedures for Evaluating Leak Detection Methods: Vapor-phase Out-of-tank Product Detectors, Technical Report, EPA Contract No. 68-03-3409, Work Assignment 02 (March 1990).

4. J. W. Maresca, Jr., N. L. Chang, Jr., and P. J. Gleckler, A Leak Detection Performance Evaluation of Automatic Tank Gauging Systems and Product Line Leak Detectors at Retail Stations, Final Report, prepared for the American Petroleum Institute, Vista Research Project 2022, Vista Research, Inc., Mountain View, California (4 January 1988).

5. J. W. Maresca, Jr., M. P. MacArthur, A. M. Regalia, J. W. Starr, C. P. Wilson, R. M. Smedfjeld, J. S. Farlow, and A. N. Tafuri, Pressure and Temperature Fluctuations in Underground Storage Tank Pipelines Containing Gasoline, *Journal of Oil and Chemical Pollution* (in press).

6. J. W. Starr and J. W. Maresca, Jr., Protocol for Evaluating Volumetric Leak Detection Methods for Underground Storage Tanks, Technical Report, contract No. 68-03-3255, Enviresponse, Inc., Livingston, New Jersey, and Vista Research, Inc., Palo Alto, California (June 1986).

7. U. S. Environmental Protection Agency, Evaluation of Volumetric Leak Detection Methods for Underground Fuel Storage Tanks, Vol. I (EPA/600/2-88/068a) and Vol. II (EPA/600/2-88/068b) Risk Reduction Engineering Laboratory, Edison, New Jersey (December 1988).

8. ASTM Subcommittee D.34.11 on Underground Storage Tanks, ASTM Practice for Evaluating and Reporting the Performance of Release Detection Systems for Underground Storage Tanks, Fifth Draft (17 August 1988).

APPENDIX A

FORM TO PRESENT A DESCRIPTION
OF THE PIPELINE LEAK DETECTION SYSTEM
EVALUATED ACCORDING TO THE EPA TEST PROCEDURE

Appendix A is the form on which to report the results of an evaluation of a pipeline leak detection system conducted according to the EPA test procedure. There are three variants of this form. The choice depends on whether the leak detection system is used as a *line tightness test*, a *monthly monitoring test*, or an *hourly test*. Use the variant that is appropriate for the system you have evaluated. If the system was evaluated as all three or any combination of these, fill out each variant that is applicable.

The appropriate variant of this form is to be filled out by the evaluating organization upon completion of the evaluation of the system. All items are to be filled out and the appropriate boxes checked. If a question is not applicable to the system, write "NA" in the appropriate space. In addition, there are seven attachments that must be filled out.

Results of the Performance Evaluation
Conducted According to EPA Test Procedures

Pipeline Leak Detection System
Used as a
Line Tightness Test

This form summarizes the results of an evaluation to determine whether the pipeline leak detection system named below and described in Attachment 1 complies with federal regulations for conducting a line tightness test. The evaluation was conducted according to the United States Environmental Protection Agency's (EPA's) evaluation procedure, specified in *Standard Test Procedures for Evaluating Leak Detection Methods: Pipeline Leak Detection Systems.* The full evaluation report includes seven attachments.

Tank system owners who use this pipeline leak detection system should keep this form on file to show compliance with the federal regulations. Tank system owners should check with state and local agencies to make sure this form satisfies the requirements of these agencies.

System Evaluated

System Name: _____

Version of System: _____

Manufacturer Name: _____

_____
(street address)

_____
(city, state, zip code)

_____
(telephone number)

_____

_____

Evaluation Results

1. The performance of this system
    ( ) meets or exceeds
    ( ) does not meet
    the federal standards established by the EPA regulation for line tightness tests.

    The EPA regulation for a line tightness test requires that the system be capable of detecting a leak as small as 0.1 gal/h with a probability of detection (P_D) of 95% and a probability of false alarm (P_{FA}) of 5%.

2. The estimated P_{FA} in this evaluation is _____% and the estimated P_D against a leak rate of 0.1 gal/h defined at a pipeline pressure of 20 psi in this evaluation is _____%.

Criterion for Declaring a Leak

3. This system
   ( ) uses a preset threshold
   ( ) measures and reports the output quantity and compares it to
       a predetermined threshold
   to determine whether the pipeline is leaking.

4. This system
   ( ) uses a single test
   ( ) uses a multiple-test sequence consisting of _____ tests (specify number of tests
       required) separated by _____ hours (specify the time interval between tests)
   to determine whether the pipeline is leaking.

5. This system declares a leak if the output of the measurement system exceeds a threshold of
   _____ (specify flow rate in gal/h) in _____ out of _____ tests (specify, for example, 1
   out of 2, 2 out of 3). Please give additional details, if necessary, in the space provided.

Evaluation Approach

6. There are five options for collecting the data used in evaluating the performance of this
   system. This system was evaluated

   ( ) at a special test facility (Option 1)
   ( ) at one or more instrumented operational storage tank facilities (Option 2)
   ( ) at five or more operational storage tank facilities verified to be tight (Option 3)
   ( ) at 10 or more operational storage tank facilities (Option 4)
   ( ) with an experimentally validated computer simulation (Option 5)

7. A total of _____ tests were conducted on nonleaking tank(s) between _____ (date)
   and _____ (date). A description of the pipeline configuration used in the evaluation is
   given in Attachment 3.

Answer questions 8 and 9 if Option 1, 2, or 5 was used.

8. The pipeline used in the evaluation was _____ in. in diameter, _____ ft long and
   constructed of _____ (fiberglass, steel, or other).

9. A mechanical line leak detector
   ( ) was
   ( ) was not
   present in the pipeline system.

Answer questions 10 and 11 if Option 3 or 4 was used.

10. The evaluation was conducted on _____ (how many) pipeline systems ranging in
    diameter from _____ in. to _____ in., ranging in length from _____ ft to
    _____ ft, and constructed of _____ (specify materials).

11. A mechanical line leak detector
   ( ) was
   ( ) was not
   present in the majority of the pipeline systems used in the evaluation.

12. Please specify how much time elapsed between the delivery of product and the start of the data collection:
   ( ) 0 to 6 h
   ( ) 6 to 12 h
   ( ) 12 to 24 h
   ( ) 24 h or more

Temperature Conditions

This system was evaluated under the range of temperature conditions specified in Table 1. The difference between the temperature of the product circulated through the pipeline for 1 h or more and the average temperature of the backfill and soil between 2 and 12 in. from the pipeline is summarized in Table 1. If Option 1, 2 or 5 was used a more detailed summary of the product temperature conditions generated for the evaluation is presented in Attachment 4. If Option 3 or 4 was used, no artificial temperature conditions were generated.

Table 1. Summary of Temperature Conditions Used in the Evaluation

Minimum Number of Conditions Required	Number of Conditions Used*	Range of ΔT (°F)**
1		$\Delta T < -25$
4		$-25 \leq \Delta T < -15$
5		$-15 \leq \Delta T < -5$
5		$-5 \leq \Delta T < +5$
5		$+5 \leq \Delta T < +15$
4		$+15 \leq \Delta T < +25$
1		$\Delta T > 25$

*This column should be filled out only if Option 1, 2, or 5 was used.

**ΔT is the difference between the temperature of the product dispensed through the pipeline for over an hour prior to the conduct of a test and the average temperature of the backfill and soil surrounding the pipe.

Data Used to Make Performance Estimates

13. The induced leak rate and the test results used to estimate the performance of this system are summarized in Attachment 5. Were any test runs removed from the data set?
   ( ) no
   ( ) yes

If yes, please specify the reason and include with Attachment 5. (If more than one test was removed, specify each reason separately.)

Sensitivity to Trapped Vapor

14. ( ) According to the vendor, this system can be used even if trapped vapor is present in the pipeline during a test.
    ( ) According to the vendor, this system *should not be used* if trapped vapor is present in the pipeline.

15. The sensitivity of this system to trapped vapor is indicated by the test results summarized in Table 2. These tests were conducted at _____ psi with _____ ml of vapor trapped in the line at a pressure of 0 psi. The data and test conditions are reported in Attachment 6.

Table 2. Summary of the Results of Trapped Vapor Tests

Test No.	ΔT (°F)	Induced Leak Rate (gal/h)	Measured Leak Rate (gal/h)
1			
2			
3			

Performance Characteristics of the Instrumentation

16. State below the performance characteristics of the primary measurement system(s) used to collect the data. (Please specify the units, for example, gallons, inches.)

    Quantity Measured: _____

    Resolution: _____

    Precision: _____

    Accuracy: _____

    Minimum Detectable Quantity: _____

    Response Time: _____

    Threshold is exceeded when the flow rate due to a leak exceeds _____ gal/h.

Application of the System

17. This leak detection system is intended to test pipeline systems that are associated with underground storage tank facilities, that contain petroleum or other chemical products, that are typically constructed of fiberglass or steel, and that typically measure 2 in. in diameter and 200 ft or less in length. The performance estimates are valid when:

    - the system that was evaluated has not been substantially changed by subsequent modifications
    - the manufacturer's instructions for using the system are followed
    - a mechanical line leak detector
      ( ) is present in
      ( ) has been removed from
      the pipeline (check both if appropriate)

- the waiting time between the last delivery of product to the underground storage tank and the start of data collection for the test is _____ h
- the waiting time between the last dispensing of product through the pipeline system and the start of data collection for the test is _____ h
- the total data collection time for the test is _____ h
- the volume of the product in the pipeline system is less than twice the volume of the product in the pipeline system used in the evaluation, unless a separate written justification for testing larger pipeline systems is presented by the manufacturer, concurred with by the evaluator, and attached to this evaluation as Attachment 8
- please give any other limitations specified by the vendor or determined during the evaluation: _____

Disclaimer: This test procedure only addresses the issue of the system's ability to detect leaks in pipelines. It does not test the equipment for safety hazards or assess the operational functionality, reliability or maintainability of the equipment.

Attachments

Attachment 1 - Description of the System Evaluated

Attachment 2 - Summary of the Performance of the System Evaluated

Attachment 3 - Summary of the Configuration of the Pipeline System(s) Used in the Evaluation

Attachment 4 - Data Sheet Summarizing Product Temperature Conditions Used in the Evaluation

Attachment 5 - Data Sheet Summarizing the Test Results and the Leak Rates Used in the Evaluation

Attachment 6 - Data Sheet Summarizing the Test Results and the Trapped Vapor Tests

Attachment 7 -- Data Sheet Summarizing the Test Results Used to Check the Relationship Supplied by the Manufacturer for Combining the Signal and Noise

Certification of Results

I certify that the pipeline leak detection system was operated according to the vendor's instructions. I also certify that the evaluation was performed according to the procedure specified by the EPA and that the results presented above are those obtained during the evaluation.

_____   _____
(name of person performing evaluation)   (organization performing evaluation)

_____   _____
(signature)   (street address)

_____   _____
(date)   (city, state, zip)

_____
(telephone number)

Pipeline Leak Detection System - Results Form

Results of the Performance Evaluation
Conducted According to EPA Test Procedures

Pipeline Leak Detection System
Used as a
Monthly Monitoring Test

This form summarizes the results of an evaluation to determine whether the pipeline leak detection system named below and described in Attachment 1 complies with federal regulations for conducting a monthly monitoring test. The evaluation was conducted according to the United States Environmental Protection Agency's (EPA's) evaluation procedure, specified in *Standard Test Procedures for Evaluating Leak Detection Methods: Pipeline Leak Detection Systems.* The full evaluation report includes seven attachments.

Tank system owners who use this pipeline leak detection system should keep this form on file to show compliance with the federal regulations. Tank system owners should check with state and local agencies to make sure this form satisfies the requirements of these agencies.

System Evaluated

System Name: _____

Version of System: _____

Manufacturer Name: _____

_____
(street address)

_____
(city, state, zip code)

_____
(telephone number)

Evaluation Results

1. The performance of this system
   ( ) meets or exceeds
   ( ) does not meet
   the federal standards established by the EPA regulation for monthly monitoring tests.

   The EPA regulation for a monthly monitoring test requires that the system be capable of detecting a leak as small as 0.2 gal/h with a probability of detection (P_D) of 95% and a probability of false alarm (P_{FA}) of 5%.

2. The estimated P_{FA} in this evaluation is _____% and the estimated P_D against a leak rate of 0.2 gal/h defined at a pipeline pressure of 20 psi in this evaluation is _____%.

Criterion for Declaring a Leak

3. This system
   ( ) uses a preset threshold
   ( ) measures and reports the output quantity and compares it to a predetermined threshold to determine whether the pipeline is leaking.

4. This system

   ( ) uses a single test
   ( ) uses a multiple-test sequence consisting of _____ tests (specify number of tests required) separated by _____ hours (specify the time interval between tests)
   to determine whether the pipeline is leaking.

5. This system declares a leak if the output of the measurement system exceeds a threshold of _____ (specify flow rate in gal/h) in _____ out of _____ tests (specify, for example, 1 out of 2, 2 out of 3). Please give additional details, if necessary, in the space povided.

   _____

   _____

   _____

Evaluation Approach

6. There are five options for collecting the data used in evaluating the performance of this system. This system was evaluated

   ( ) at a special test facility (Option 1)
   ( ) at one or more instrumented operational storage tank facilities (Option 2)
   ( ) at five or more operational storage tank facilities verified to be tight (Option 3)
   ( ) at 10 or more operational storage tank facilities (Option 4)
   ( ) with an experimentally validated computer simulation (Option 5)

7. A total of _____ tests were conducted on nonleaking tank(s) between _____ (date) and _____ (date). A description of the pipeline configuration used in the evaluation is given in Attachment 3.

Answer questions 8 and 9 if Option 1, 2, or 5 was used.

8. The pipeline used in the evaluation was _____ in. in diameter, _____ ft long and constructed of _____ (fiberglass, steel, or other).

9. A mechanical line leak detector
   ( ) was
   ( ) was not
   present in the pipeline system.

Answer questions 10 and 11 if Option 3 or 4 was used.

10. The evaluation was conducted on _____ (how many) pipeline systems ranging in diameter from _____ in. to _____ in., ranging in length from _____ ft to _____ ft, and constructed of _____ (specify materials).

11. A mechanical line leak detector
   ( ) was
   ( ) was not
   present in the majority of the pipeline systems used in the evaluation.

12. Please specify how much time elapsed between the delivery of product and the start of the data collection:
   ( ) 0 to 6 h
   ( ) 6 to 12 h
   ( ) 12 to 24 h
   ( ) 24 h or more

Temperature Conditions

This system was evaluated under the range of temperature conditions specified in Table 1. The difference between the product circulated through the pipeline for 1 h or more and the average temperature of the backfill and soil between 2 and 12 in. from the pipeline is summarized in Table 1. If Option 1, 2 or 5 was used a more detailed summary of the product temperature conditions generated for the evaluation is presented in Attachment 4. If Option 3 or 4 was used, no artificial temperature conditions were generated

Table 1. Summary of Temperature Conditions Used in the Evaluation

Minimum Number of Conditions Required	Number of Conditions Used*	Range of ΔT (°F)**
1		$\Delta T < -25$
4		$-25 \leq \Delta T < -15$
5		$-15 \leq \Delta T < -5$
5		$-5 \leq \Delta T < +5$
5		$+5 \leq \Delta T < +15$
4		$+15 \leq \Delta T < +25$
1		$\Delta T > 25$

*This column should be filled out only if Option 1, 2, or 5 was used.

**ΔT is the difference between the temperature of the product dispensed through the pipeline for over an hour prior to the conduct of a test and the average temperature of the backfill and soil surrounding the pipe.

Data Used to Make Performance Estimates

13. The induced leak rate and the test results used to estimate the performance of this system are summarized in Attachment 5. Were any test runs removed from the data set?
   ( ) no
   ( ) yes

   If yes, please specify the reason and include with Attachment 5. (If more than one test was removed, specify each reason separately.)

Sensitivity to Trapped Vapor

14. ( ) According to the vendor, this system can be used even if trapped vapor is present in the pipeline during a test.
    ( ) According to the vendor, this system *should not be used* if trapped vapor is present in the pipeline.

15. The sensitivity of this system to trapped vapor is indicated by the test results summarized in Table 2. These tests were conducted at _____ psi with _____ ml of vapor trapped in the line at a pressure of 0 psi. The data and test conditions are reported in Attachment 6.

Table 2. Summary of the Results of Trapped Vapor Tests

Test No.	ΔT ("F)	Induced Leak Rate (gal/h)	Measured Leak Rate (gal/h)
1			
2			
3			

Performance Characteristics of the Instrumentation

16. State below the performance characteristics of the primary measurement system used to collect the data. (Please specify the units, for example, gallons, inches.)

    Quantity Measured: _____

    Resolution: _____

    Precision: _____

    Accuracy: _____

    Minimum Detectable Quantity: _____

    Response Time: _____

    Threshold is exceeded when the flow rate due to a leak exceeds _____ gal/h.

Application of the System

17. This leak detection system is intended to test pipeline systems that are associated with underground storage tank facilities, that contain petroleum or other chemical products, that are typically constructed of fiberglass or steel, and that typically measure 2 in. in diameter and 150 ft or less in length. The performance estimates are valid when:

    - the system that was evaluated has not been substantially changed by subsequent modifications
    - the manufacturer's instructions for using the system are followed
    - the mechanical line leak detector
      ( ) is present in
      ( ) has been removed from
      the pipeline (check both if appropriate)

- the waiting time between the last delivery of product to the underground storage tank and the start of data collection for the test is _____ h
- the waiting time between the last dispensing of product through the pipeline system and the start of data collection for the test is _____ h
- the total data collection time for the test is _____ h
- the volume of the product in the pipeline is less than twice the volume of the product in the pipeline system used in the evaluation, unless separate written justification for testing larger pipeline systems is presented by the manufacturer, concurred with by the evaluator, and attached to this evaluation as Attachment 8
- please give any other limitations specified by the vendor or determined during the evaluation: _____

_____

Disclaimer: This test procedure only addresses the issue of the system's ability to detect leaks in pipelines. It does not test the equipment for safety hazards or assess the operational functionality, reliability or maintainability of the equipment.

Attachments

Attachment 1 - Description of the System Evaluated

Attachment 2 - Summary of the Performance of the System Evaluated

Attachment 3 - Summary of the Configuration of the Pipeline System(s) Used in the Evaluation

Attachment 4 - Data Sheet Summarizing Product Temperature Conditions Used in the Evaluation

Attachment 5 - Data Sheet Summarizing the Test Results and the Leak Rates Used in the Evaluation

Attachment 6 - Data Sheet Summarizing the Test Results and the Trapped Vapor Tests

Attachment 7 - Data Sheet Summarizing the Test Results Used to Check the Relationship Supplied by the Manufacturer for Combining the Signal and Noise

Certification of Results

I certify that the pipeline leak detection system was operated according to the vendor's instructions. I also certify that the evaluation was performed according to the procedure specified by the EPA and that the results presented above are those obtained during the evaluation.

_____   _____
(name of person performing evaluation)   (organization performing evaluation)

_____   _____
(signature)   (street address)

_____   _____
(date)   (city, state, zip)

_____
(telephone number)

Results of the Performance Evaluation
Conducted According to EPA Test Procedures

Pipeline Leak Detection System
Used as an
Hourly Test

This form summarizes the results of an evaluation to determine whether the pipeline leak detection system named below and described in Attachment 1 complies with federal regulations for conducting an hourly test. The evaluation was conducted according to the United States Environmental Protection Agency's (EPA's) evaluation procedure, specified in *Standard Test Procedures for Evaluating Leak Detection Methods: Pipeline Leak Detection Systems.* The full evaluation report includes seven attachments.

Tank system owners who use this pipeline leak detection system should keep this form on file to show compliance with the federal regulations. Tank system owners should check with state and local agencies to make sure this form satisfies the requirements of these agencies.

System Evaluated

System Name: _____

Version of System: _____

Manufacturer Name: _____

_____
(street address)

_____
(city, state, zip code)

_____
(telephone number)

Evaluation Results

1. The performance of this system
    ( ) meets or exceeds
    ( ) does not meet
    the federal standards established by the EPA regulation for hourly tests.

    The EPA regulation for an hourly test requires that the system be capable of detecting a leak as small as 3.0 gal/h with a probability of detection (P_D) of 95% and a probability of false alarm (P_{FA}) of 5%.

2. The estimated P_{FA} in this evaluation is _____ % and the estimated P_D against a leak rate of 3.0 gal/h defined at a pipeline pressure of 20 psi in this evaluation is _____ %.

Criterion for Declaring a Leak

3. This system
    ( ) uses a preset threshold
    ( ) measures and reports the output quantity and compares it to a predetermined threshold to determine whether the pipeline is leaking.

4. This system
    ( ) uses a single test
    ( ) uses a multiple-test sequence consisting of _____ tests (specify number of tests required) separated by _____ hours (specify the time interval between tests) to determine whether the pipeline is leaking.

5. This system declares a leak if the output of the measurement system exceeds a threshold of _____ (specify flow rate in gal/h) in _____ out of _____ tests (specify, for example, 1 out of 2, 2 out of 3). If more detail is required, please specify in the space provided.

    _____
    _____

Evaluation Approach

6. There are five options for collecting the data used in evaluating the performance of this system. This system was evaluated

    ( ) at a special test facility (Option 1)
    ( ) at one or more instrumented operational storage tank facilities (Option 2)
    ( ) at five or more operational storage tank facilities verified to be tight (Option 3)
    ( ) at 10 or more operational storage tank facilities (Option 4)
    ( ) with an experimentally validated computer simulation (Option 5)

7. A total of _____ tests were conducted on nonleaking tank(s) between _____ (date) and _____ (date). A description of the pipeline configuration used in the evaluation is summarized in Attachment 3.

Answer questions 8 and 9 if Option 1, 2, or 5 was used.

8. The pipeline used in the evaluation was _____ in. in diameter, _____ ft long and constructed of _____ (fiberglass, steel, or other).

9. A mechanical line leak detector
    ( ) was
    ( ) was not
    present in the pipeline system.

Answer questions 10 and 11 if Option 3 or 4 was used.

10. The evaluation was conducted on _____ (how many) pipeline systems ranging in diameter from _____ in. to _____ in., ranging in length from _____ ft to _____ ft, and constructed of _____ (specify materials).

11. A mechanical line leak detector
   ( ) was
   ( ) was not
   present in the majority of the pipeline systems used in the evaluation.

12. Please specify how much time elapsed between the delivery of product and the start of the data collection:
   ( ) 0 to 6 h
   ( ) 6 to 12 h
   ( ) 12 to 24 h
   ( ) 24 h or more

Temperature Conditions

This system was evaluated under the range of temperature conditions specified in Table 1. The difference between the temperature of the product circulated through the pipeline for 1 h or more and the average temperature of the backfill and soil between 2 and 12 in. from the pipeline is summarized in Table 1. If Option 1, 2 or 5 was used, a more detailed summary of the product temperature conditions generated for the evaluation is presented in Attachment 4. If Option 3 or 4 was used, no artificial temperature conditions were generated.

Table 1. Summary of Temperature Conditions Used in the Evaluation

Minimum Number of Conditions Required	Number of Conditions Used*	Range of ΔT (°F)**
1		$\Delta T < -25$
4		$-25 \leq \Delta T < -15$
5		$-15 \leq \Delta T < -5$
5		$-5 \leq \Delta T < +5$
5		$+5 \leq \Delta T < +15$
4		$+15 \leq \Delta T < +25$
1		$\Delta T > 25$

*This column should be filled out only if Option 1, 2, or 5 was used.

**ΔT is the difference between the temperature of the product dispensed through the pipeline for over an hour prior to the conduct of a test and the average temperature of the backfill and soil surrounding the pipe.

Data Used to Make Performance Estimates

13. The induced leak rate and the test results used to estimate the performance of this system are summarized in Attachment 5. Were any test runs removed from the data set?
   ( ) no
   ( ) yes

   If yes, please specify the reason and include with Attachment 5. (If more than one test was removed, specify each reason separately.)

Sensitivity to Trapped Vapor

14. ( ) According to the vendor, this system can be used even if trapped vapor is present in the pipeline during a test.
    ( ) According to the vendor, this system *should not be used* if trapped vapor is present in the pipeline.

15. The sensitivity of this system to trapped vapor is indicated by the test results summarized in Table 2. These tests were conducted at _____ psi with _____ ml of vapor trapped in the line at a pressure of 0 psi. The data and test conditions are reported in Attachment 6.

Table 2. Summary of the Results of Trapped Vapor Tests

Test No.	ΔT (°F)	Induced Leak Rate (gal/h)	Measured Leak Rate (gal/h)
1			
2			
3			

Performance Characteristics of the Instrumentation

16. State below the performance characteristics of the primary measurement system used to collect the data. (Please specify the units, for example, gallons, inches.)

    Quantity Measured: _____

    Resolution: _____

    Precision: _____

    Accuracy: _____

    Minimum Detectable Quantity: _____

    Response Time: _____

    Threshold is exceeded when the flow rate due to a leak exceeds _____ gal/h.

Application of the System

17. This leak detection system is intended to test pipeline systems that are associated with underground storage tank facilities, that contain petroleum or other chemical products, that are typically constructed of fiberglass or steel, and that typically measure 2 in. in diameter and 150 ft or less in length. The performance estimates are valid when:

    - the system that was evaluated has not been substantially changed by subsequent modifications
    - the manufacturer's instructions for using the system are followed
    - the mechanical line leak detector
      ( ) is present in
      ( ) has been removed from
      the pipeline (check both if appropriate)

- the waiting time between the last delivery of product to the underground storage tank and the start of data collection for the test is _____ h
- the waiting time between the last dispensing of product through the pipeline system and the start of data collection for the test is _____ h
- the total data collection time for the test is _____ h
- the volume of the product in the pipeline is less than twice the volume of the product in the pipeline system used in the evaluation, unless separate written justification for testing larger pipeline systems is presented by the manufacturer, concurred with by the evaluator, and attached to this evaluation as Attachment 8
- please give any other limitations specified by the vendor or determined during the evaluation: _____

Disclaimer: This test procedure only addresses the issue of the system's ability to detect leaks in pipelines. It does not test the equipment for safety hazards or assess the operational functionality, reliability or maintainability of the equipment.

Attachments

Attachment 1 - Description of the System Evaluated

Attachment 2 - Summary of the Performance of the System Evaluated

Attachment 3 - Summary of the Configuration of the Pipeline System(s) Used in the Evaluation

Attachment 4 - Data Sheet Summarizing Product Temperature Conditions Used in the Evaluation

Attachment 5 - Data Sheet Summarizing the Test Results and the Leak Rates Used in the Evaluation

Attachment 6 - Data Sheet Summarizing the Test Results and the Trapped Vapor Tests

Attachment 7 - Data Sheet Summarizing the Test Results Used to Check the Relationship Supplied by the Manufacturer for Combining the Signal and Noise

Certification of Results

I certify that the pipeline leak detection system was operated according to the vendor's instructions. I also certify that the evaluation was performed according to the procedure specified by the EPA and that the results presented above are those obtained during the evaluation.

_____   _____
(name of person performing evaluation)   (organization performing evaluation)

_____   _____
(signature)   (street address)

_____   _____
(date)   (city, state, zip)

_____
(telephone number)

APPENDIX B

ATTACHMENTS 1 THROUGH 7 TO THE FORM IN APPENDIX A

Appendix B comprises the seven attachments to the form in Appendix A.

In Attachment 1 you are asked to describe the pipeline leak detection system by answering 26 questions, most of which are multiple-choice.

In Attachment 2, you are asked to present a summary of performance estimates by filling in the tables provided. Like the form in Appendix A, Attachment 2 has three variants, depending on whether the leak detection system is used as a *line tightness test*, a *monthly monitoring test*, or an *hourly test*. Choose the variant that is appropriate for the system you have evaluated. In addition, if your system uses a multiple-test strategy, please fill out that part of Attachment 2 which asks for the results of the first test in the sequence.

In Attachment 3, you are asked to summarize the configuration of the pipeline system(s) used in the evaluation. The charts that are provided are broken down according to the options selected for the evaluation. For example, if the system was evaluated at a specialized test facility, at an instrumented operational UST facility, or by computer simulation, fill out the chart marked "Options 1, 2 and 5." If the system was evaluated at five operational UST facilities whose integrity had been verified, fill in the chart marked "Option 3." If the system was evaluated at 10 or more operational UST facilities, use the chart marked "Option 4."

In Attachment 4, you are asked to summarize the temperature conditions used in the evaluation. Again, the charts are broken down according to the options selected for the evaluation.

In Attachments 5 and 6, you are asked to summarize the leak rates and the trapped vapor tests, respectively. You are also asked to summarize the results of the tests performed. The charts provided are organized similarly to those in Attachment 4.

In Attachment 7, you are asked to summarize the test results that are used to check the relationship provided by the manufacturer, which describes how the signal adds to the noise.

Description

Pipeline Leak Detection System

This form provides supporting information on the operating principles of the leak detection system or on how the equipment works. This form is to be filled out by the evaluating organization with assistance from the manufacturer before the start of the evaluation.

Describe the important features of the system as indicated below. A detailed description is not required, nor is it necessary to reveal proprietary features of the system.

To minimize the time required to complete this form, the most frequently expected answers to the questions have been provided. For those answers that are dependent on site conditions, please give answers that apply in "typical" conditions. Please write in any additional information about the system that you believe is important.

Check all appropriate boxes for each question. Check more than one box per question if it applies. If 'Other' is checked, please complete the space provided to specify or briefly describe the matter. If necessary, use all the white space next to a question to complete a description.

System Name and Version: _____

Date: _____

Applicability of the System

1. With what products can this system be used? (Check all applicable responses.)

    ( ) gasoline
    ( ) diesel
    ( ) aviation fuel
    ( ) fuel oil #4
    ( ) fuel oil #6
    ( ) solvent
    ( ) waste oil
    ( ) other (specify) _____

2. What types of pipelines can be tested? (Check all applicable responses.)

    ( ) fiberglass
    ( ) steel
    ( ) other (specify) _____

3. Can this leak detection system be used to test double-wall pipeline systems?

    ( ) yes   ( ) no

4. What is the nominal diameter of a pipeline that can be tested with this system?

   ( ) 1 in. or less
   ( ) between 1 and 3 in.
   ( ) between 3 and 6 in.
   ( ) between 6 and 10 in.
   ( ) other _____

5. The system can be used on pipelines pressurized to _____ psi.

   The safe maximum operating pressure for this system is _____ psi.

6. Does the system conduct a test while a mechanical line leak detector is in place in the pipeline?

   ( ) yes   ( ) no

General Features of the System

7. What type of test is the system conducting? (Check all applicable responses.)

   ( ) 0.1 gal/h Line Tightness Test
   ( ) 0.2 gal/h Monthly Monitoring Test
   ( ) 3 gal/h Hourly Test

8. Is the system permanently installed on the pipeline?

   ( ) yes   ( ) no

   Does the system test the line automatically?

   ( ) yes   ( ) no

   If a leak is declared, what does the system do? (Check all applicable responses.)

   ( ) displays or prints a message
   ( ) triggers an alarm
   ( ) alerts the operator
   ( ) shuts down the dispensing system

9. What quantity or quantities are measured by the system? (Please list.)

   _____
   _____
   _____

10. Does the system use a preset threshold that is automatically activated or that automatically turns on an alarm?

   ( ) yes (If yes, skip question 11.)
   ( ) no (If no, answer question 11.)

11. Does the system measure and report the quantity?

   ( ) yes   ( ) no

If so, is the output quantity converted to flow rate in gallons per hour?

( ) yes   ( ) no

12. What is the specified line pressure during a test?

( ) operating pressure of line
( ) 150% of operating pressure
( ) a specific test pressure of _____ psi

Test Protocol

13. What is the minimum waiting period required between a delivery of product to an underground storage tank and the start of the data collection for a pipeline leak detection test?

( ) no waiting period
( ) less than 15 min
( ) 15 min to 1 h
( ) 1 to 5 h
( ) 6 to 12 h
( ) 12 to 24 h
( ) greater than 24 h
( ) variable (Briefly explain.) _____

14. What is the minimum waiting period required between the last dispensing of product through the pipeline and the start of the data collection for a pipeline leak detection test?

( ) no waiting period
( ) less than 15 min
( ) 15 min to 1 h
( ) 1 to 4 h
( ) 4 to 8 h
( ) greater than 8 h
( ) variable (Briefly explain.) _____

15. What is the minimum amount of time necessary to set up equipment and complete a leak detection test? (Include setup time, waiting time and data collection time. If a multiple-test sequence is used, give the amount of time necessary to complete the first test as well as the total amount of time necessary to complete the entire sequence.)

_____ h (single test)
_____ h (multiple test)

16. Does the system compensate for those pressure or volume changes of the product in the pipeline that are due to temperature changes?

( ) yes   ( ) no

17. Is there a special test to check the pipeline for trapped vapor?

( ) yes   ( ) no

18. Can a test be performed with trapped vapor in the pipeline?

( ) yes   ( ) no

19. If trapped vapor is found in the pipeline, is it removed before a test is performed?

( ) yes   · ( ) no

20. Are deviations from this protocol acceptable?

( ) yes   ( ) no ·

If yes, briefly specify: _____

_____

_____

21. Are elements of the test procedure determined by on-site testing personnel?

( ) yes   ( ) no

If yes, which ones? (Check all applicable responses.)

( ) waiting period between filling the tank and the beginning of data
    collection for the test

( ) length of test

( ) determination of the presence of vapor pockets

( ) determination of "outlier" (or anomalous) data that may be discarded

( ) other (Describe briefly.) _____

Data Acquisition

22. How are the test data acquired and recorded?

( ) manually

( ) by strip chart

( ) by computer

( ) by microprocessor

23. Certain calculations are necessary to reduce and analyze the data. How are these calculations done?

( ) manual calculations by the operator on site

( ) interactive computer program used by the operator

( ) automatically done with a computer program

( ) automatically done with a microprocessor

Detection Criterion

24. What threshold is used to determine whether the pipeline is leaking?

_____ (in the units used by the measurement system)

_____ (in gal/h)

25. Is a multiple-test sequence used to determine whether the pipeline is leaking?

    ( ) yes (If yes, answer the three questions below)
    ( ) no (If no, skip the three questions below)

    How many tests are conducted? _____

    How many tests are required before a leak can be declared? _____

    What is the time between tests? _____

    (Enter 0 if the tests are conducted one after the other.)

Calibration

26. How frequently are the sensor systems calibrated?

    ( ) never
    ( ) before each test
    ( ) weekly
    ( ) monthly
    ( ) semi-annually
    ( ) yearly or less frequently

Summary of Performance Estimates

Pipeline Leak Detection System
Used as a
Line Tightness Test

Complete this page if the pipeline leak detection system has been evaluated as a line tightness test. Please complete the first table. Completion of the last three tables is optional. (The last three tables present the performance of the system for different combinations of thresholds, probabilities of false alarm, and probabilities of detection. They are useful for comparing the performance of this system to that of other systems.)

Performance of the Pipeline Leak Detection System as Evaluated

Description	Leak Rate (gal/h)	P_D	P_{FA}	Threshold (gal/h)
Evaluated System	0.10			
EPA Standard	0.10	0.95	0.05	N/A

Probability of False Alarm as a Function of Threshold

Threshold (gal/h)	Probability of False Alarm
	0.10
	0.075
	0.05
	0.05

Probability of Detection as a Function of Threshold for a Leak Rate of 0.10 gal/h

Threshold (gal/h)	Probability of Detection
	0.95
	0.90
	0.80
	0.50

Smallest Leak Rate That Can Be Detected with the Specified Probability of Detection and Probability of False Alarm

Leak Rate (gal/h)	Probability of Detection	Probability of False Alarm
	0.95	0.10
	0.95	0.075
	0.95	0.05
	0.90	0.05
	0.80	0.05
	0.50	0.05

Attachment 2

Summary of Performance Estimates

Pipeline Leak Detection System
Used as a
Monthly Monitoring Test

Complete this page if the pipeline leak detection system has been evaluated as a monthly monitoring test. Please complete the first table. Completion of the last three tables is optional. (The last three tables present the performance of the system for different combinations of thresholds, probabilities of false alarm, and probabilities of detection. They are useful for comparing the performance of this system to that of other systems.)

Performance of the Pipeline Leak Detection System as Evaluated

Description	Leak Rate (gal/h)	P_D	P_{FA}	Threshold (gal/h)
Evaluated System	0.20			
EPA Standard	0.20	0.95	0.05	N/A

Probability of False Alarm as a Function of Threshold

Threshold (gal/h)	Probability of False Alarm
	0.10
	0.075
	0.05
	0.05

Probability of Detection as a Function of Threshold for a Leak Rate of 0.20 gal/h

Threshold (gal/h)	Probability of Detection
	0.95
	0.90
	0.80
	0.50

Smallest Leak Rate that Can Be Detected with the Specified Probability of Detection and Probability of False Alarm

Leak Rate (gal/h)	Probability of Detection	Probability of False Alarm
	0.95	0.10
	0.95	0.075
	0.95	0.05
	0.90	0.05
	0.80	0.05
	0.50	0.05

Summary of Performance Estimates

Pipeline Leak Detection System
Used as a
Line Tightness Test
First Test of a Multiple-Test Sequence

Complete these tables only if the system being evaluated requires, as part of its test protocol, more than one complete test to determine whether the pipeline is leaking. System performance based on the first test alone must be reported on this form. Please complete the first table. Completion of the last three tables is optional. (The last three tables present the performance of the system for different combinations of thresholds, probabilities of false alarm, and probabilities of detection. They are useful for comparing the performance of this system to that of other systems.)

Performance of the Pipeline Leak Detection System as Evaluated

Description	Leak Rate (gal/h)	P_D	P_{FA}	Threshold (gal/h)
Evaluated System	0.10			
EPA Standard	0.10	0.95	0.05	N/A

Probability of False Alarm as a Function of Threshold

Threshold (gal/h)	Probability of False Alarm
	0.10
	0.075
	0.05
	0.05

Probability of Detection as a Function of Threshold for a Leak Rate of 0.10 gal/h

Threshold (gal/h)	Probability of Detection
	0.95
	0.90
	0.80
	0.50

Smallest Leak Rate that Can Be Detected with the Specified Probability of Detection and Probability of False Alarm

Leak Rate (gal/h)	Probability of Detection	Probability of False Alarm
	0.95	0.10
	0.95	0.075
	0.95	0.05
	0.90	0.05
	0.80	0.05
	0.50	0.05

Summary of Performance Estimates

Pipeline Leak Detection System
Used as a
Monthly Monitoring Test
First Test of a Multiple-Test Sequence

Complete these tables only if the system being evaluated requires, as part of its test protocol, more than one complete test to determine whether the pipeline is leaking. System performance based on the first test alone must be reported on this form. Please complete the first table. Completion of the last three tables is optional. (The last three tables present the performance of the system for different combinations of thresholds, probabilities of false alarm, and probabilities of detection. They are useful for comparing the performance of this system to that of other systems.)

Performance of the Pipeline Leak Detection System as Evaluated

Description	Leak Rate (gal/h)	P_D	P_{FA}	Threshold (gal/h)
Evaluated System	0.20			
EPA Standard	0.20	0.95	0.05	N/A

Probability of False Alarm as a Function of Threshold

Threshold (gal/h)	Probability of False Alarm
	0.10
	0.075
	0.05
	0.05

Probability of Detection as a Function of Threshold for a Leak Rate of 0.20 gal/h

Threshold (gal/h)	Probability of Detection
	0.95
	0.90
	0.80
	0.50

Smallest Leak Rate that Can Be Detected with the Specified Probability of Detection and Probability of False Alarm

Leak Rate (gal/h)	Probability of Detection	Probability of False Alarm
	0.95	0.10
	0.95	0.075
	0.95	0.05
	0.90	0.05
	0.80	0.05
	0.50	0.05

Attachment 2
Summary of Performance Estimates
Pipeline Leak Detection System
Used as an
Hourly Test

Complete this page if the pipeline leak detection system has been evaluated as an hourly test. Please complete the first table. Completion of the last three tables is optional. (The last three tables present the performance of the system for different combinations of thresholds, probabilities of false alarm, and probabilities of detection. They are useful for comparing the performance of this system to that of other systems.)

Performance of the Pipeline Leak Detection System as Evaluated

Description	Leak Rate (gal/h)	P_D	P_{FA}	Threshold (gal/h)
Evaluated System	3.0			
EPA Standard	3.0	0.95	0.05	N/A

Probability of False Alarm as a Function of Threshold

Threshold (gal/h)	Probability of False Alarm
	0.10
	0.075
	0.05
	0.05

Probability of Detection as a Function of Threshold for a Leak Rate of 3.0 gal/h

Threshold (gal/h)	Probability of Detection
	0.95
	0.90
	0.80
	0.50

Smallest Leak Rate that Can Be Detected with the Specified Probability of Detection and Probability of False Alarm

Leak Rate (gal/h)	Probability of Detection	Probability of False Alarm
	0.95	0.10
	0.95	0.075
	0.95	0.05
	0.90	0.05
	0.80	0.05
	0.50	0.05

Summary of Performance Estimates

Pipeline Leak Detection System
Used as an
Hourly Test
First Test of a Multiple-Test Sequence

Complete this page only if the system being evaluated requires, as part of its test protocol, more than one complete test to determine whether the pipeline is leaking. System performance based on the first test alone must be reported on this form. Please complete the first table. Completion of the last three tables is optional. (The last three tables present the performance of the system for different combinations of thresholds, probabilities of false alarm, and probabilities of detection. They are useful for comparing the performance of this system to that of other systems.)

Performance of the Pipeline Leak Detection System as Evaluated

Description	Leak Rate (gal/h)	P_D	P_{FA}	Threshold (gal/h)
Evaluated System	3.0			
EPA Standard	3.0	0.95	0.05	N/A

Probability of False Alarm as a Function of Threshold

Threshold (gal/h)	Probability of False Alarm
	0.10
	0.075
	0.05
	0.05

Probability of Detection as a Function of Threshold for a Leak Rate of 3.0 gal/h

Threshold (gal/h)	Probability of Detection
	0.95
	0.90
	0.80
	0.50

Smallest Leak Rate that Can Be Detected with the Specified Probability of Detection and Probability of False Alarm

Leak Rate (gal/h)	Probability of Detection	Probability of False Alarm
	0.95	0.10
	0.95	0.075
	0.95	0.05
	0.90	0.05
	0.80	0.05
	0.50	0.05

Attachment 3

Summary of the Configuration of the Pipeline System(s) Used in the Evaluation

Pipeline Leak Detection System
Options 1, 2, and 5

Specialized Test Facility, Operational Storage Tank System, or Computer Simulation	
Inside diameter of pipeline (in.)	
Length of pipeline (tank to dispenser) (ft)	
Volume of product in line during testing (gal)	
Type of material (fiberglass, steel, other[1])	
Type of product in tank and pipeline (gasoline, diesel, other[2])	
Was a mechanical line leak detector present? (yes or no)	
Was trapped vapor present? (yes or no)	
Bulk Modulus (B) (psi)	
B/V_o (psi/ml)	
Storage tank capacity (gal)	

[1] Specify type of construction materal.
[2] Specify type of product for each tank.

Attachment 3

Summary of the Configuration of the Pipeline System(s) Used in the Evaluation

Pipeline Leak Detection System
Option 3

Operational Storage Tank System	1	2	3	4	5
Inside diameter of pipeline (in.)					
Length of pipeline (tank to dispenser) (ft)					
Volume of product in line during testing (gal)					
Type of material (fiberglass, steel, other[1])					
Type of product in pipeline (gasoline, diesel, other[2])					
Was a mechanical line leak detector present? (yes or no)					
Was trapped vapor present? (yes or no)					
Bulk Modulus (B) (psi)					
B/V$_o$ (psi/ml)					
Storage tank capacity (gal)					

[1] Specify type of construction material.
[2] Specify type of product for each tank.

Operational Storage Tank System	6	7	8	9	10
Inside diameter of pipeline (in.)					
Length of pipeline (tank to dispenser) (ft)					
Volume of product in line during testing (gal)					
Type of material (fiberglass, steel, other[1])					
Type of product in pipeline (gasoline, diesel, other[2])					
Was a mechanical line leak detector present? (yes or no)					
Was trapped vapor present? (yes or no)					
Bulk Modulus (B) (psi)					
B/V$_o$ (psi/ml)					
Storage tank capacity (gal)					

[1] Specify type of construction material.
[2] Specify type of product for each tank.

Attachment 3

Summary of the Configuration of the Pipeline System(s)
Used in the Evaluation

Pipeline Leak Detection System
Option 4

Operational Storage Tank System	1	2	3	4	5
Inside diameter of pipeline (in.)					
Length of pipeline (tank to dispenser) (ft)					
Volume of product in line during testing (gal)					
Type of material (fiberglass, steel, other[1])					
Type of product in pipeline (gasoline, diesel, other[2])					
Was a mechanical line leak detector present? (yes or no)					
Was trapped vapor present? (yes or no)					
Bulk Modulus (B) (psi)					
B/V_o (psi/ml)					
Storage tank capacity (gal)					

[1] Specify type of construction material.
[2] Specify type of product for each tank.

Operational Storage Tank System	6	7	8	9	10
Inside diameter of pipeline (in.)					
Length of pipeline (tank to dispenser) (ft)					
Volume of product in line during testing (gal)					
Type of material (fiberglass, steel, other[1])					
Type of product in pipeline (gasoline, diesel, other[2])					
Was a mechanical line leak detector present? (yes or no)					
Was trapped vapor present? (yes or no)					
Bulk Modulus (B) (psi)					
B/V_o (psi/ml)					
Storage tank capacity (gal)					

[1] Specify type of construction material.
[2] Specify type of product for each tank.

Summary of the Configuration of the Pipeline System(s) Used in the Evaluation

Pipeline Leak Detection System
Option 4

Operational Storage Tank System	11	12	13	14	15
Inside diameter of pipeline (in.)					
Length of pipeline (tank to dispenser) (ft)					
Volume of product in line during testing (gal)					
Type of material (fiberglass, steel, other[1])					
Type of product in pipeline (gasoline, diesel, other[2])					
Was a mechanical line leak detector present? (yes or no)					
Was trapped vapor present? (yes or no)					
Bulk Modulus (B) (psi)					
B/V_o (psi/ml)					
Storage tank capacity (gal)					

[1] Specify type of construction material.
[2] Specify type of product for each tank.

Operational Storage Tank System	16	17	18	19	20
Inside diameter of pipeline (in.)					
Length of pipeline (tank to dispenser) (ft)					
Volume of product in line during testing (gal)					
Type of material (fiberglass, steel, other[1])					
Type of product in pipeline (gasoline, diesel, other[2])					
Was a mechanical line leak detector present? (yes or no)					
Was trapped vapor present? (yes or no)					
Bulk Modulus (B) (psi)					
B/V_o (psi/ml)					
Storage tank capacity (gal)					

[1] Specify type of construction material.
[2] Specify type of product for each tank.

Attachment 4

Data Sheet Summarizing the Product Temperature Conditions Used in the Evaluation

Pipeline Leak Detection System
Options 1 and 5

Test No. (Based on Temperature Condition)	Date Test Began	Nominal Product Temperature before Circulation Was Started	Time Circulation Started	Time Circulation Ended	Duration of Circulation	Time of Temperature Measurements	T_{TB}	T_1	T_2	T_3	T_G	$T_{TB} - T_G$	Temperature Test Matrix Category
	(D-M-Y)	(°F)	(local military)	(°F)	(h-min)	(local military)	(°F)	(°F)	(°F)	(°F)	(°F)	(°F)	(Table 5.1)
1													
2													
3													
4													
5													
6													
7													
8													
9													
10													
11													
12													
13													
14													
15													

Data Sheet Summarizing the Product Temperature Conditions Used in the Evaluation

Pipeline Leak Detection System
Options 1 and 5

Test No. (Based on Temperature Condition)	Date Test Began	Nominal Product Temperature before Circulation Was Started	Time Circulation Started	Time Circulation Ended	Duration of Circulation	Time of Temperature Measurements	T_{TB}	T_1	T_2	T_3	T_G	$T_{TB} - T_G$	Temperature Test Matrix Category
	(D-M-Y)	(°F)	(local military)	(°F)	(h-min)	(local military)	(°F)	(°F)	(°F)	(°F)	(°F)	(°F)	(Table 5.1)
16													
17													
18													
19													
20													
21													
22													
23													
24													
25													
26													
27													
28													
29													
30													
31													
32													
33													
34													
35													

Attachment 4

Data Sheet Summarizing the Product Temperature Conditions Used in the Evaluation

Pipeline Leak Detection System
Option 2

Test No. (Based on Temperature Condition)	Date Test Began	Date of Last Product Delivery	Time of Last Product Delivery	Time between Product Delivery and Data Collection for Test	Time of Last Dispensing	Time between Last Dispensing and Start of Data Collection for Test	Time of Temperature Measurements	T_{TB}	T_1	T_2	T_3	T_G	$T_{TB} - T_G$	Temperature Test Matrix Category
	(D-M-Y)	(D-M-Y)	(local military)	(h-min)	(local military)	(h-min)	(local military)	(°F)	(°F)	(°F)	(°F)	(°F)	(°F)	(Table 5.1)
1														
2														
3														
4														
5														
6														
7														
8														
9														
10														
11														
12														
13														
14														
15														
16														
17														
18														

Data Sheet Summarizing the Product Temperature Conditions Used in the Evaluation

Pipeline Leak Detection System
Option 2

Test No. (Based on Temperature Condition)	Date Test Began	Date of Last Product Delivery	Time of Last Product Delivery	Time between Product Delivery and Data Collection for Test	Time of Last Dispensing	Time between Last Dispensing and Start of Data Collection for Test	Time of Temperature Measurements	T_{TB}	T_1	T_2	T_3	T_G	$T_{TB} - T_G$	Temperature Test Matrix Category
	(D-M-Y)	(D-M-Y)	(local military)	(h-min)	(local military)	(h-min)	(local military)	(°F)	(°F)	(°F)	(°F)	(°F)	(°F)	(Table 5.1)
19														
20														
21														
22														
23														
24														
25														
26														
27														
28														
29														
30														
31														
32														
33														
34														
35														

Attachment 5
Data Sheet Summarizing the Test Results and the Leak Rates Used in the Evaluation
Pipeline Leak Detection System
Options 1 and 5

Test No. (Based on Temperature Condition)	Date Test Began	Induced Leak Rate	Time between End of Circulation and Start of Data Collection for Test	Time Data Collection Began	Time Data Collection Ended	Measured Test Result	Was Threshold Exceeded?
	(D-M-Y)	(gal/h)	(h-min)	(local military)	(local military)	(gal/h)	(yes or no)
1							
2							
3							
4							
5							
6							
7							
8							
9							
10							
11							
12							
13							
14							
15							
16							
17							
18							
19							
20							
21							
22							
23							
24							
25							
26							
27							
28							
29							
30							
31							
32							
33							

(Table heading: Test No. 1)

Data Sheet Summarizing the Test Results and the Leak Rates Used in the Evaluation

Pipeline Leak Detection System
Options 1 and 5

Test No. (Based on Temperature Condition)	Date Test Began	Induced Leak Rate	Time between End of Circulation and Start of Data Collection for Test	Time Data Collection Began	Time Data Collection Ended	Measured Test Result	Was Threshold Exceeded?
Test No. 2							
	(D-M-Y)	(gal/h)	(h-min)	(local military)	(local military)	(gal/h)	(yes or no)
1							
2							
3							
4							
5							
6							
7							
8							
9							
10							
11							
12							
13							
14							
15							
16							
17							
18							
19							
20							
21							
22							
23							
24							
25							
26							
27							
28							
29							
30							
31							
32							
33							

Data Sheet Summarizing the Test Results and the Leak Rates Used in the Evaluation

Pipeline Leak Detection System
Options 1 and 5

Test No.							
Test No. (Based on Temperature Condition)	**Date Test Began**	**Induced Leak Rate**	**Time between End of Circulation and Start of Data Collection for Test**	**Time Data Collection Began**	**Time Data Collection Ended**	**Measured Test Result**	**Was Threshold Exceeded?**
	(D-M-Y)	(gal/h)	(h-min)	(local military)	(local military)	(gal/h)	(yes or no)
1							
2							
3							
4							
5							
6							
7							
8							
9							
10							
11							
12							
13							
14							
15							
16							
17							
18							
19							
20							
21							
22							
23							
24							
25							
26							
27							
28							
29							
30							
31							
32							
33							

Data Sheet Summarizing the Test Results and the Leak Rates Used in the Evaluation

Pipeline Leak Detection System
Options 1 and 5

				Test No. 4				
Test No. (Based on Temperature Condition)	Date Test Began	Induced Leak Rate	Time between End of Circulation and Start of Data Collection for Test	Time Data Collection Began	Time Data Collection Ended	Measured Test Result	Was Threshold Exceeded?
	(D-M-Y)	(gal/h)	(h-min)	(local military)	(local military)	(gal/h)	(yes or no)
1							
2							
3							
4							
5							
6							
7							
8							
9							
10							
11							
12							
13							
14							
15							
16							
17							
18							
19							
20							
21							
22							
23							
24							
25							
26							
27							
28							
29							
30							
31							
32							
33							

Attachment 5

Data Sheet Summarizing the Test Results and the Leak Rates Used in the Evaluation

Pipeline Leak Detection System
Option 2

Test No. 1								
Test No. (Based on Temperature Condition)	Date Test Began	Induced Leak Rate	Time between Product Delivery and Data Collection for Test	Time between Last Dispensing and Start of Data Collection for Test	Time Data Collection Began	Time Data Collection Ended	Measured Test Result	Was Threshold Exceeded?
	(D-M-Y)	(gal/h)	(h-min)	(h-min)	(local military)	(local military)	(gal/h)	(yes or no)
1								
2								
3								
4								
5								
6								
7								
8								
9								
10								
11								
12								
13								
14								
15								
16								
17								
18								
19								
20								
21								
22								
23								
24								
25								
27								
28								
29								
30								
31								
32								
33								

Data Sheet Summarizing the Test Results and the Leak Rates Used in the Evaluation

Pipeline Leak Detection System
Option 2

Test No. (Based on Temperature Condition)	Date Test Began	Induced Leak Rate	Time between Product Delivery and Data Collection for Test	Time between Last Dispensing and Start of Data Collection for Test	Time Data Collection Began	Time Data Collection Ended	Measured Test Result	Was Threshold Exceeded?
	(D-M-Y)	(gal/h)	(h-min)	(h-min)	(local military)	(local military)	(gal/h)	(yes or no)
1								
2								
3								
4								
5								
6								
7								
8								
9								
10								
11								
12								
13								
14								
15								
16								
17								
18								
19								
20								
21								
22								
23								
24								
25								
27								
28								
29								
30								
31								
32								
33								

Test No. 2

Attachment 5
(continued)
Data Sheet Summarizing the Test Results and the Leak Rates Used in the Evaluation
Pipeline Leak Detection System
Option 2

Test No. (Based on Temperature Condition)	Date Test Began	Induced Leak Rate	Time between Product Delivery and Data Collection for Test	Time between Last Dispensing and Start of Data Collection for Test	Time Data Collection Began	Time Data Collection Ended	Measured Test Result	Was Threshold Exceeded?
	(D-M-Y)	(gal/h)	(h-min)	(h-min)	(local military)	(local military)	(gal/h)	(yes or no)
1								
2								
3								
4								
5								
6								
7								
8								
9								
10								
11								
12								
13								
14								
15								
16								
17								
18								
19								
20								
21								
22								
23								
24								
25								
27								
28								
29								
30								
31								
32								
33								

Test No. 3

Attachment 5
(concluded)

Data Sheet Summarizing the Test Results and the Leak Rates Used in the Evaluation

Pipeline Leak Detection System
Option 2

					Test No. 4			
Test No. (Based on Temperature Condition)	Date Test Began	Induced Leak Rate	Time between Product Delivery and Start of Data Collection for Test	Time between Last Dispensing and Start of Data Collection for Test	Time Data Collection Began	Time Data Collection Ended	Measured Test Result	Was Threshold Exceeded?
	(D-M-Y)	(gal/h)	(h-min)	(h-min)	(local military)	(local military)	(gal/h)	(yes or no)
1								
2								
3								
4								
5								
6								
7								
8								
9								
10								
11								
12								
13								
14								
15								
16								
17								
18								
19								
20								
21								
22								
23								
24								
25								
27								
28								
29								
30								
31								
32								
33								

Attachment 5

Data Sheet Summarizing the Test Results and the Leak Rates Used in the Evaluation

Pipeline Leak Detection System
Options 3 and 4

Test No. (Based on Temperature Condition)	Date Test Began	Date of Last Product Delivery	Time of Last Product Delivery	Time between Product Delivery and Start of Data Collection for Test	Time of Last Dispensing	Time between Last Dispensing and Start of Data Collection for Test	Time Data Collection Began	Time Data Collection Ended	Measured Test Result	Was Threshold Exceeded?
	(D-M-Y)	(D-M-Y)	(local military)	(h-min)	(local military)	(h-min)	(local military)	(local military)	(gal/h)	(yes or no)
1										
2										
3										
4										
5										
6										
7										
8										
9										
10										
11										
12										
13										
14										
15										

Data Sheet Summarizing the Test Results and the Leak Rates Used in the Evaluation

Pipeline Leak Detection System
Options 3 and 4

Test No. (Based on Temperature Condition)	Date Test Began	Date of Last Product Delivery	Time of Last Product Delivery	Time between Product Delivery and Start of Data Collection for Test	Time of Last Dispensing	Time between Last Dispensing and Start of Data Collection for Test	Time Data Collection Began	Time Data Collection Ended	Measured Test Result	Was Threshold Exceeded?
	(D-M-Y)	(D-M-Y)	(local military)	(h-min)	(local military)	(h-min)	(local military)	(local military)	(gal/h)	(yes or no)
16										
17										
18										
19										
20										
21										
22										
23										
24										
25										
26										
27										
28										
29										
30										
31										
32										
33										
34										
35										

Attachment 6

Data Sheet Summarizing the Test Results and the Trapped Vapor Tests

Pipeline Leak Detection System
Options 1 and 5

Summary of Temperature Conditions

Test No.	Date Test Began	Nominal Product Temperature before Circulation Was Started	Time Circulation Started	Time Circulation Ended	Duration of Circulation	Time of Temperature Measurements	T_{TB}	T_1	T_2	T_J	T_G	$T_{TB} \cdot T_G$	Temperature Test Matrix Category
	(D-M-Y)	(°F)	(local military)	(local military)	(h-min)	(local military)	(°F)	(°F)	(°F)	(°F)	(°F)	(°F)	(Table 5.1)
1													
2													
3													

Summary of Leak Rates

Test No.	Date Test Began	Pipeline Pressure	Induced Leak Rate	Time between End of Circulation and Start of Data Collection for Test	Time Data Collection Began	Time Data Collection Ended	Measured Test Result	Was Threshold Exceeded?
	(D-M-Y)	(psi)	(gal/h)	(h-min)	(local military)	(local military)	(gal/h)	(yes or no)
1								
2								
3								

Attachment 6

Data Sheet Summarizing the Test Results and the Trapped Vapor Tests

Pipeline Leak Detection System
Option 2

Summary of Temperature Conditions

Test No.	Date Test Began	Date of Last Product Delivery	Time of Last Product Delivery	Time between Product Delivery and Start of Data Collection for Test	Time of Last Dispensing	Time between Start of Data Collection for Test and Last Dispensing	Time of Temperature Measurements	T_{TB}	T_1	T_2	T_3	T_G	$T_{TB} - T_G$	Temperature Test Matrix Category
	(D-M-Y)	(D-M-Y)	(local military)	(h-min)	(local military)	(h-min)	(local military)	(°F)	(°F)	(°F)	(°F)	(°F)	(°F)	(Table 5.1)
1														
2														
3														

Summary of Leak Rates

Test No.	Date Test Began	Pipeline Pressure	Induced Leak Rate	Time between Product Delivery and Start of Data Collection for Test	Time between Start of Data Collection for Test and Last Dispensing	Time Data Collection Began	Time Data Collection Ended	Measured Test Result	Was Threshold Exceeded?
	(D-M-Y)	(psi)	(gal/h)	(h-min)	(h-min)	(local military)	(local military)	(gal/h)	(yes or no)
1									
2									
3									

Attachment 7

Data Sheet Summarizing the Test Results Used to Check the Relationship Supplied by the Manufacturer for Combining the Signal and Noise

Pipeline Leak Detection System
Options 1 and 5

First Check		
Test No.	Actual Leak Rate* (gal/h)	Measured Leak Rate (gal/h)
1		
2		
3		
4		
5		
6		

* Recommended leak rates for monthly monitoring tests and line tightness tests: 0.0, 0.05, 0.10, 0.20, 0.30 and 0.40 gal/h. Recommended leak rates for hourly tests: 0.0, 2.0, 2.5, 3.0, 3.5, and 4.0 gal/h.

Second Check		
Test No.	Actual Leak Rate* (gal/h)	Measured Leak Rate (gal/h)
A		
B		
C		
A + B*		

* A + B is the summation of the results of Tests A and B using the manufacturer's relationship for combining the signal and the noise.

APPENDIX C

Protocol Notification Form

I have received a copy of *Standard Test Procedures for Evaluating Leak Detection Methods: Pipeline Leak Detection Systems* and would like to be placed on a mailing list in case changes or modifications are made to this document.

Name: _____

Title: _____

Company: _____

Address: _____
      (Street)

_____
      (City, State, Zip)

Telephone: _____

Mail this form to:

        Office of Underground Storage Tanks
        U.S. Environmental Protection Agency
        Attention: Pipeline Evaluation Protocol
        401 M Street, S. W.
        Mail Stop OS-410
        Washington, D.C. 20460

APPENDIX D

Random Selection of Leak Rates

Condition No. 1		Condition No. 2		Condition No. 3		Condition No. 4		Condition No. 5		Condition No. 6		Condition No. 7	
Test No.	Leak Rate (gal/h)	Test No.	Leak Rate (gal/h)	Test No.	Leak Rate (gal/h)	Test No.	Leak Rate (gal/h)	Test No.	Leak Rate (gal/h)	Test No.	Leak Rate (gal/h)	Test No.	Leak Rate (gal/h)
1	0.31	1	0.20	1	0.12	1	0.46	1	0.22	1	0.39	1	0.12
2	0.18	2	0.21	2	0.11	2	0.36	2	0.31	2	0.23	2	0.37
3	0.39	3	0.25	3	0.11	3	0.23	3	0.42	3	0.26	3	0.26
4	0.35	4	0.49	4	0.28	4	0.17	4	0.48	4	0.43	4	0.29
5	0.33	5	0.37	5	0.42	5	0.15	5	0.42	5	0.11	5	0.44

Condition No. 8		Condition No. 9		Condition No. 10		Condition No. 11		Condition No. 12		Condition No. 13		Condition No. 14	
Test No.	Leak Rate (gal/h)	Test No.	Leak Rate (gal/h)	Test No.	Leak Rate (gal/h)	Test No.	Leak Rate (gal/h)	Test No.	Leak Rate (gal/h)	Test No.	Leak Rate (gal/h)	Test No.	Leak Rate (gal/h)
1	0.28	1	0.35	1	0.34	1	0.25	1	0.45	1	0.11	1	0.49
2	0.41	2	0.13	2	0.14	2	0.40	2	0.10	2	0.41	2	0.15
3	0.49	3	0.16	3	0.35	3	0.18	3	0.31	3	0.15	3	0.42
4	0.47	4	0.46	4	0.34	4	0.37	4	0.30	4	0.12	4	0.49
5	0.24	5	0.23	5	0.20	5	0.30	5	0.42	5	0.45	5	0.21

Condition No. 15		Condition No. 16		Condition No. 17		Condition No. 18		Condition No. 19		Condition No. 20		Condition No. 21	
Test No.	Leak Rate (gal/h)	Test No.	Leak Rate (gal/h)	Test No.	Leak Rate (gal/h)	Test No.	Leak Rate (gal/h)	Test No.	Leak Rate (gal/h)	Test No.	Leak Rate (gal/h)	Test No.	Leak Rate (gal/h)
1	0.18	1	0.26	1	0.12	1	0.16	1	0.45	1	0.21	1	0.24
2	0.33	2	0.25	2	0.38	2	0.33	2	0.39	2	0.33	2	0.34
3	0.28	3	0.21	3	0.15	3	0.46	3	0.22	3	0.30	3	0.41
4	0.34	4	0.14	4	0.45	4	0.49	4	0.16	4	0.14	4	0.27
5	0.35	5	0.45	5	0.21	5	0.40	5	0.41	5	0.17	5	0.25

APPENDIX E

STATISTICS

This appendix defines the statistical calculations that must be made in the protocol and presents a simple example using only five data points to illustrate the calculations. Many of the commercially available spreadsheets and most mathematical calculators have a function with which to calculate the mean and standard deviation from a set of data and to fit a least-squares line to these data. The confidence intervals can be easily calculated once the mean and standard deviation are known.

Mean and Standard Deviation

When a collection of data is being analyzed, it is often useful to examine the average value of the data and the spread of the data around that average. These two data qualities are given numerically by the mean and the standard deviation.

The mean, or the average, of a set of data is generally denoted by a bar over the data variable, e.g., $\bar{x}$, and is calculated as

$$\bar{x} = \frac{\sum_{i=1}^{N} x_i}{N} = \frac{x_1 + x_2 + x_3 + \ldots + x_N}{N},$$

where N is the number of data samples and x_i is the ith data sample. Σ is the symbol used to represent the summation.

The standard deviation, denoted by s, measures the spread around the mean and is calculated by

$$s = \sqrt{\frac{\sum_{i=1}^{N} (x_i - \bar{x})^2}{N-1}}.$$

This equation is sometimes seen in an alternate form as

$$s = \sqrt{N \cdot \frac{\overline{x^2} - (\bar{x})^2}{N-1}},$$

where $(\bar{x})^2$ is the square of the mean of the data and $\overline{x^2}$ is the mean of the squared data. An example of these calculations is given in Table E.1. (Sometimes the standard deviation is calculated with N instead of N - 1 in the denominator.)

Table E.1. Example of Mean and Standard Deviation Calculations

i	x_i	$(x_i - \bar{x})^2$	$(x_i)^2$
1	83	16	6,889
2	90	9	8,100
3	94	49	8,836
4	86	1	7,396
N=5	82	25	6,724
Sum	435	100	37,945
Mean	87		7,589
Standard Deviation	$5 = \sqrt{\frac{100}{5-1}} = 5.0$ or $= \sqrt{5 \cdot \frac{7.589 - (87)^2}{5-1}} = 5.0$		

Confidence Intervals on the Mean and Standard Deviation

The confidence interval on a quantity is the range of values which are not statistically different from a specific value of the quantity. For example, if the confidence interval on a mean of 2.0 is from 1.7 to 2.5, a measured mean within the range of 1.7 to 2.5 is not statistically different from a mean of 2.0. The confidence intervals on the mean and on the standard deviation are calculated with the t distribution and the χ^2 distribution, respectively.

To calculate the 95% confidence interval on a mean, $\bar{x}$, of N samples, we first use a t-distribution table (found in any basic statistics book) to determine the value of t for $\alpha = 0.05$ and for degrees of freedom equal to N - 1. If the standard deviation of these N samples is s, the confidence interval is given by

$$\bar{x} \pm \frac{s \cdot t}{\sqrt{N}}.$$

For N = 5, the value of the t-statistic for a one-tailed test is 2.78. The lower and upper confidence intervals on the mean for the data shown in Table E.1 are 80.784 and 93.216, respectively.

To calculate the 95% confidence interval on the standard deviation, we first use a χ^2-distribution table to determine the values of χ^2 for $\alpha = 0.05$ and for $1 - \alpha = 0.95$, both for N - 1 degrees of freedom. The lower limit of the confidence interval is then given by

$$\sqrt{\frac{N \cdot s^2}{\chi^2_{0.05}}}$$

and the upper limit is given by

$$\sqrt{\frac{N \cdot s^2}{\chi^2_{0.95}}}.$$

Values for the χ^2-distribution can be obtained in the appendices of most statistics textbooks. The lower and upper confidence intervals on the standard deviation for the data shown in Table E.1 are 3.627 and 13.259, where $\chi^2_{0.05} = 9.500$ and $\chi^2_{0.95} = 0.711$ for 4 degrees of freedom.

Linear Regression Analysis: Least-squares Fit

In studying the relationship between two measured quantities, it is desirable to derive from experimental data an equation that best expresses this relationship. For cases in which the data seem to be linearly related, a *best fit* to the data is obtained by using the linear regression method of least squares.

Let the ith value of the independent data variable be x_i and the corresponding dependent data variable be y_i. Then, the linear relationship between x and y is given by

$$y = mx + b$$

where

$$m = \frac{\frac{1}{N}\left(\sum_{i=1}^{N} x_i y_i\right) - \overline{x}\,\overline{y}}{\overline{x^2} - (\overline{x})^2}$$

$$b = \frac{\overline{y}\,\overline{x^2} - \frac{1}{N}\left(\sum_{i=1}^{N} x_i y_i\right)\overline{x}}{\overline{x^2} - (\overline{x})^2}$$

and N is the number of data pairs. (For an explanation of $\overline{x}$, see the section at the beginning of this appendix entitled Mean and Standard Deviation).

Two different quantities are used as a measure of the accuracy of the linear fit. The first is the variance* along the regression line given by

$$s^2 = \frac{\sum_{i=1}^{N} y_i^2 - b\sum_{i=1}^{N} y_i - m\sum_{i=1}^{N} x_i y_i}{N - 2}.$$

The second measure of the accuracy is the variance of the slope given by

$$s_m^2 = \frac{N S^2}{N \sum_{i=1}^{N} (x_i^2) - \left(\sum_{i=1}^{N} x\right)^2}.$$

A least-squares line was fit to the data in Table E.1; the results show that m = -0.600, b = 88.800, s = 5.699, and s_m = 1.793. An x-y plot of the data shown in Table E.1 will show that the data are not modeled well by a line.

---

* The variance is simply the standard deviation squared.